STOP DOOM SPENDING

The 6-Week Plan to Stop Impulse Spending, Ease Money Anxiety, and Build a Wealth Mindset in Just **15 Minutes a Day** — No Spreadsheets Needed

Tali Moss

CONTENTS

INTRODUCTION:

This book translates the behavioral-finance research I studied while earning my degree in finance into plain-English daily steps. Every tool you'll use in the next six weeks, like pause techniques, dopamine resets, friction walls, comes straight from the same science that guides modern investing and consumer-behavior analysis. Think of this as the bridge between what researchers know and what the rest of us actually do with our money. Now, let's dive in...

Money. Everyone needs it, everybody wants it, nobody talks about it honestly, and almost everyone feels like they're screwing it up. You might have a decent paycheck and still wonder where the hell it went by the end of the week. You might open your banking app and immediately want to throw your phone into Grand Canyon. Or maybe you've convinced yourself you're "bad with money," while quietly hoping your future self somehow figures it out before retirement.

I'll tell you what: you're not dumb. You're not lazy. You're not doomed. Your brain is just wired for a world that no longer exists.

Once upon a time, our brains were obsessed with survival: food, safety, and not getting eaten. Fast-forward to today and those same survival instincts are trying to navigate TikTok doom-spending trends, Buy Now Pay Later buttons, and influencers unboxing $700 skincare fridges. No wonder you're swiping your card like it's a stress-relief tool. Doom spending, panic spending, "treat yourself" spending — it's all the same brain wiring, just in a shinier, faster, more expensive package.

And it works… for about five minutes. You get that tiny dopamine high, that "hell yeah, life isn't so bad" moment when you hit Place Order. Then the regret shows up. Then the shame. Then the cycle starts again. Buy → Regret → Shame → Repeat. Congratulations, you're human.

The financial industry wants you to believe it's all discipline. Budget harder. Stop drinking lattes. Cancel Netflix. Live like a monk until you die. Which is both depressing and wrong. If it was really about discipline, half of Wall Street wouldn't be panic-selling every time the market sneezes.

Money isn't just math. It's psychology. It's habit loops, fear triggers, childhood scripts, and cultural noise. If you don't understand how your brain plays you, no spreadsheet in the world will save you.

That's what this book is about: **hacking your brain so it stops screwing with your wallet.**

Here's what you're going to get:

- Why your brain falls for traps like money dysmorphia and anchoring (aka "50% off is still 100% a trick").
- How to interrupt spending urges with tactics that actually work in the real world, not just on paper.
- A way to look at your money without spiraling into anxiety (just so you know: it's one simple dashboard, not twelve apps).
- A six-week reset plan that gives you micro wins, not burnout.
- And maybe most importantly: the identity shift from "I'm bad with money" to "I'm calm, capable, and building wealth without the drama."

This isn't another book that tells you to give up joy and eat beans for life. It's not a lecture from someone who's never panic-bought three $30 candles after a bad day. And it's not a guilt trip. It's a reset. A practical, psychology-based way to get your money and your brain playing on the same team.

By the end of these pages, **you won't just know how money works, you'll know how you work.** You'll stop feeling like your wallet is a black hole and start feeling like you can breathe again.

No shame. No spreadsheets of death. No "cut coffee" lectures. Just you, your brain, and a system that actually sticks.

Because you were never "bad with money." You were just working with the wrong manual.

PART I:

Why Your Brain Sabotages Your Wallet

Chapter 1:

Doom Spending, Money Dysmorphia & Other Modern Money Traps

What Doom Spending Really Is (and Why TikTok Made It Famous)

Picture this: the world feels like it's on fire, your inbox is a war zone, and you're emotionally held together by caffeine and denial. Instead of screaming into the void, you scroll, you click, and there you go, there's a package on the way. New shoes. A candle. A weird gadget that slices avocado three ways. Do you need it? Absolutely not. Does it fix your existential dread? For about twelve seconds, yes.

That's doom spending.

TikTok made the term famous, but the behavior has been around forever. Doom spending is retail therapy's dramatic cousin. It's buying things you don't need, not out of joy, but out of low-key despair. It's the "I hate my job and the planet is melting, so I deserve this" purchase. It's the "life is too short, I'm getting the expensive sushi" swipe. It's spending as a pressure valve, a way to channel all the chaos into something you can control.

And it's addictive as hell.

Here's why: when you buy something, your brain rewards you with a dopamine hit. Tiny, quick, satisfying. The problem is that the hit wears off, leaving the original stress still sitting there, plus a fresh layer of guilt for spending money you didn't have. So the cycle goes: **doom → buy → dopamine → regret → shame → repeat.**

And modern life pours gasoline on this cycle. One-click checkouts, Buy Now Pay Later apps, and "your package is on its way!" emails all spike that dopamine loop. Marketers know this. Social media knows this. The entire economy knows this. Which means your brain is up against billion-dollar systems designed to keep you swiping.

So no, doom spending isn't you being "bad with money." It's your nervous system doing its best with crappy tools. Fear, scarcity, and anxiety trigger the same survival circuits that once helped our ancestors hoard food before winter. The difference? You're not storing nuts in a cave, you're panic-buying a Dyson vacuum on Afterpay.

I know, a little doom spending here and there isn't the end of the world. Everyone panic-buys dumb shit sometimes (if you've never blacked out on Amazon and woken up to find a package of glow-in-the-dark coasters on your porch, congratulations, you're a unicorn). The real problem is when doom spending becomes the default, your go-to coping strategy for stress, boredom, or hopelessness. That's when it snowballs into debt, money dysmorphia, and the constant feeling that you're never safe, no matter how much you earn.

In other words, doom spending is less about the candle you bought and more about the story your brain is telling: *"I can't handle reality, so I'll buy myself an escape."* The escape is temporary. The bill is not.

But here's the good news: once you see doom spending for what it really is, **a glitch in your brain's coping system,** you can start to hack it. You can build better tools, better defaults, and better ways to ride out the chaos without torching your wallet.

This chapter, as well as this whole first section of the book, is about dragging those money traps into the light. Doom spending is just the opening act. Next up? Money dysmorphia, the buy-regret-shame cycle, and the sneaky little death spiral called Buy Now Pay Later.

But first, sit with this truth: You're not doomed because you doom-spend. You're just overdue for an upgrade in how you deal with life's chaos.

The Illusion of Scarcity: Understanding Money Dysmorphia

You've heard of body dysmorphia… it's when people see flaws in the mirror that aren't actually there. Money dysmorphia is the financial version of that. It's when you *feel* broke even if you're not, or when you convince yourself you're "doing fine" while your credit card balance is quietly plotting your downfall.

It's that moment when you get paid and suddenly you feel rich, so you order UberEats three nights in a row… only to feel crushed and "poor again" by the weekend. It's scrolling through Instagram and deciding your perfectly functional apartment is a dungeon because someone else your age bought a house in a different zip code. It's opening your banking app, seeing actual money there, and still feeling unsafe.

Money dysmorphia is not about the numbers, it's about perception. And **perception lies.**

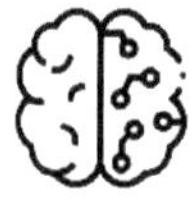

Psychology

Our brains are terrible at judging "enough." We're wired for scarcity because, historically, not having enough could literally kill us. Your brain doesn't care that you've got direct deposit and Woolies down the street; it's still running on prehistoric coding. It's scanning for danger and whispering, *"What if it runs out? What if it's never enough?"* That whisper turns into anxiety, even when the numbers are okay.

On the flip side, money dysmorphia can also trick you into reckless confidence. Ever had $200 left after paying bills and felt like Jeff Bezos? That's dysmorphia too. Your brain inflates the number, convinces you you've got "room," and next thing you know you've spent $250 on a weekend bender plus brunch.

Modern life makes this worse.

- **Social media**: You compare your behind-the-scenes to everyone else's highlight reel.
- **Cost-of-living rollercoaster**: Groceries double in price, rent skyrockets, wages crawl. Your brain doesn't know whether to panic or pretend.
- **Childhood money messages**: If you grew up hearing "we can't afford that," you might carry that scarcity ghost into adulthood, even if you're making decent money now.

The result? You're living in a distorted reality. You're never quite sure where you stand. You feel broke when you're not, safe when you shouldn't, and anxious no matter what.

That's money dysmorphia. And it's exhausting.

The danger isn't just emotional; it's behavioral. When you *feel* broke, you may cling to money so tightly you never invest, which means your future self gets screwed. When you *feel* flush, you overspend, which means your future self also gets screwed. Dysmorphia pushes you to make short-term emotional choices instead of calm, reality-based ones.

Let's reframe: the problem isn't that you don't have enough — the problem is that **you don't have clarity**. Scarcity is often an illusion, but it feels real because your brain hates uncertainty. The cure isn't doubling your salary overnight (though, hey, if you can swing that, go for it). The cure is building a way to see reality without the distortion.

DEEP DIVE

In a 2022 APA survey, **42 percent** of millennials reported that social-media exposure directly worsened their sense of financial adequacy.

The brain treats "likes" tied to purchases as micro-rewards, reinforcing distorted self-assessment.

Tracking emotional triggers after scrolling sessions can help reset that distortion loop.

Later in this book, we'll build your **Reality Dashboard** — a one-page snapshot of your actual money picture. No vibes. No illusions. Just data that calms the panic and shuts down the false confidence.

For now, just notice the pattern. The next time you say "I'm broke," ask: *Am I really, or is this dysmorphia talking?* Because nine times out of ten, your bank account isn't lying, your brain is.

The Emotional Cycle of Buy → Regret → Shame → Repeat

Here goes the world's worst hangover: the Amazon hangover. You know the one… the package arrives, and instead of excitement, you feel dread. You rip open the box, stare at the random gadget you panic-bought at midnight, and wonder, *"Who the hell ordered this? Was it me? Was I drunk? Possessed?"* Congrats: you've just completed the buy → regret → shame cycle.

Here's how it plays out:

Step 1: Buy.

You're stressed, tired, lonely, bored, or all of the above. Your brain screams, *"Fix it!"* and spending feels like the quickest fix. Click, swipe, tap, and boom, dopamine hits. For a fleeting moment, life feels lighter.

Step 2: Regret.

The dopamine wears off faster than a cheap sugar high. Reality creeps in: the bill, the overdraft, the mental math of "how am I going to make rent if I keep this up?" Now the purchase that felt like a solution feels like a problem.

Step 3: Shame.

Here comes the gut punch: *"Why am I like this? Why can't I get it together? I'm just bad with money."* That shame doesn't motivate you to stop, instead it actually makes you want another hit of dopamine, because shame feels awful and you'll do anything to escape it. Which means…

Step 4: Repeat.

The worse you feel, the more tempting it is to buy something else. Another coffee. Another online order. Another "small" treat that adds up. And around you go again, like a hamster on a very expensive wheel.

Sound familiar? That's because this cycle is addictive by design. Every step reinforces the next, training your brain like Pavlov's dog. Stress triggers the urge to buy. Buying gives you temporary relief. Regret kicks in. Shame deepens. And the quickest way out of shame? You guessed it: buy something else.

And the cycle doesn't care about the amount. It could be a $5 iced latte or a $500 handbag. The mechanics are the same. You're not paying for the item, **you're paying for the feeling**. And feelings fade.

Here's the psychological loop in plain terms:

- **Dopamine:** "Yes, this will fix everything!"
- **Cortisol:** "Oh shit, it didn't fix anything."
- **Shame spiral:** "You're a disaster, let's not talk about it."
- **Dopamine again:** "New plan — this next purchase will definitely fix it."

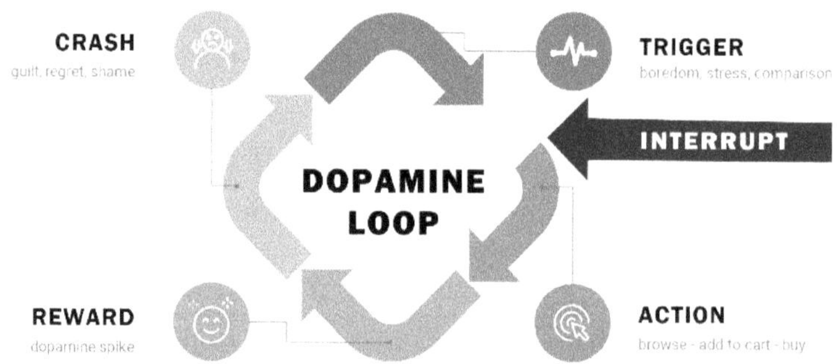

Every impulsive purchase runs through this loop. **Our goal is to interrupt it at the trigger point**, before dopamine takes the wheel.

Marketers know this cycle intimately. That's why your inbox is full of "flash sale ending soon" emails. That's why social media feeds you ads *just when you're most vulnerable.* They're not just selling products, they're selling your brain another round of the cycle.

The problem with that is you can't shop your way out of stress. But you *can* break the loop by recognizing it for what it is: a pattern, not a personal failing. Once you see the hamster wheel, you can step off. Later in this book, I'll give you the exact tactics to interrupt the cycle — from the **10-Second Pause** to **Wishlist Wednesday,** so the next time stress comes knocking, your first response isn't "add to cart."

DEEP DIVE

Neuro-imaging studies show that post-purchase regret activates the same brain regions as **physical pain** (insula and anterior cingulate).

Understanding that your crash isn't "weak willpower" but a normal dopamine-withdrawal response helps replace shame with strategy: pause, label, and reset.

For now, in this section we are just noticing things. So, the next time you feel that urge rising, pause and ask: *Am I about to buy the thing, or am I about to buy the feeling?*

Because nine times out of ten, you're not craving the item. You're craving relief. And relief can come from a lot cheaper places than Amazon.

The Hidden Costs of Buy Now, Pay Later (BNPL Creep)

"Four easy payments of $19.99." Sounds harmless, right? It's not $80, it's *just* $20 today. That's basically free. Until, of course, you realize you've got five different BNPL plans running at once, and suddenly half your paycheck is spoken for before it even lands.

That's BNPL creep — the slow, sneaky way Buy Now, Pay Later turns into Pay Forever, Never Free.

Here's why it works: BNPL isn't just a payment option. It's a psychological trick. It takes the sting out of the purchase by **disconnecting the pleasure of buying from the pain of paying**. Your brain goes, *"Hell yeah, I get the shoes now and deal with the bill later."* Later-you, of course, hates now-you for this arrangement. But now-you doesn't care.

And it's everywhere. Clothes, tech, makeup, food delivery, you can Afterpay your lunch at this point. Companies love it because it makes you spend more. According to industry research cited by Forbes, consumers spend 10–40% more per transaction when using BNPL compared to paying in full. That's not an accident. It's a feature.

The danger isn't the single payment. It's the creep. You don't feel the weight of $200 when it's broken into four payments. You don't panic over $20 here, $30 there. But stack a few of those across multiple apps, and suddenly you're juggling payments like a circus act. You're not even sure what you owe anymore, just that something's always coming out of your account.

And that's the emotional cost: BNPL keeps you in a constant state of owing. There's no finish line, no "all clear." Even if the amounts are small, the mental load of always having micro-debts hanging over you creates background anxiety. You might not consciously think about it, but your nervous system feels it: a low hum of *"I'm never caught up."*

BNPL also trains your brain to normalize living on credit. It tells you: *"Affordability isn't about what you have, it's about what you can spread out."* Which works until an unexpected bill hits and your "easy payments" suddenly aren't so easy anymore. That's how people end up maxing out, missing payments, tanking credit scores, all from what felt like harmless little $20 slices.

To be clear: BNPL isn't evil in itself. Used sparingly, it can be fine. The issue is when it becomes invisible, when your default is to defer pain until future-you is drowning. That's the creep.

So here's the **rule of thumb**: if you wouldn't buy it with one full payment today, don't slice it into four. Because whether you pay in one hit or four, you're still buying the same thing, and if it wasn't worth $80 upfront, it sure as hell isn't worth $20 x 4 with extra stress attached.

BNPL isn't just a financial trap. It's a psychological one. And it thrives on the same brain wiring we've already covered: instant gratification, distorted perception, shame loops. Recognize it, call it out, and you're halfway free already.

Now, if you've ever wondered why you're extra vulnerable to these traps, here's the curiosity for you: they don't come out of nowhere. The way you spend, save, and panic around money didn't start with Afterpay. It started way earlier… in your family, your culture, and your personal history.

Case File 01

Daniel vs. BNPL

Daniel was 29, a freelance designer who swore he "only used Afterpay for small stuff." When we mapped it out, he had **seven active BNPL accounts** totalling **$1,240 in rolling micro-debt**, none of which ever felt like debt because each app only showed its own sliver.

His trigger pattern was textbook *present bias*: a stress spike → scroll → "just four payments of $19.99." The pleasure hit was immediate; the cost felt imaginary. When he finally faced the math, he realized he was losing nearly **$80 a week** to interest-free "little things."

We built a simple friction wall: he **deleted all BNPL apps**, set up a **Cart Quarantine** folder on his browser, and created a **Future-Self Fund** where $40 auto-transferred each Friday, the same amount he'd usually waste.

Three months later, Daniel had **zero BNPL debt**, **$520 saved**, and reported fewer 2 a.m. shopping spirals. His words: "It's weird, I still get the dopamine, but now it's from checking my balance, not the mailbox."

And to flip it fully, we have to zoom out. Because none of these habits happen in a vacuum. The way you spend, save, and stress about money has roots — in your family, your culture, your past. Which brings us to Chapter 2.

Chapter 2:

Your Financial Flashpoints

(Family, Trauma, and Culture)

How Childhood Money Messages Shape Adult Behavior

Nobody grows up money-neutral. Whether your parents were savers, spenders, or full-blown financial chaos agents, you absorbed it. Even if no one sat you down and said, "Here's how money works," you got the message loud and clear — through fights, habits, or silence.

Think back. Maybe you heard:

- *"We can't afford that."* (Translation: money is always scarce.)
- *"Do you think I'm made of money?"* (Translation: asking is greedy, wanting is shameful.)
- *"Money isn't everything."* (Translation: but secretly, it's the thing we stress about constantly.)
- *"Don't talk about money."* (Translation: money is taboo, keep your questions to yourself.)

None of these are lessons in compound interest, but they sure as hell stick.

If you grew up in a house where bills were always a fight, you may now avoid opening your own mail. If your parents treated credit cards like Monopoly money, you may repeat that pattern, or go to the opposite extreme, refusing debt even when it could help you. If your family praised "self-sacrifice," you may struggle to spend even when you can afford to.

Psychologists call these **money scripts** — unconscious beliefs about money, usually formed before age 10, that keep running the show decades later. They don't have to be logical. They just have to be familiar.

For example:

- **Saver kids:** If you grew up with parents who pinched pennies, you might be financially secure now but unable to enjoy it. You hoard money because spending feels unsafe, even on things you value.
- **Spender kids:** If shopping was how your family coped with stress, you may repeat that as an adult. Bad day? Target run. Heartbreak? New shoes. Loneliness? BNPL spree.
- **Silent households:** If money was never discussed, you may have zero framework as an adult. You don't know if you're "good" or "bad" with money, you just feel anxious all the time.
- **Status households:** If success was measured in stuff, you may be chasing upgrades forever, nicer car, bigger house, better vacations, and never feel satisfied.

None of this is destiny. But it does explain why smart adults keep making baffling money choices. They're not making decisions in the present, they're reenacting childhood scripts on repeat.

And here's something mind-blowing: kids don't hear, *"We can't afford that right now because Dad just lost a client and cash flow is tight."* They hear, *"We can never afford anything. Money is scary. Wanting things is bad."* That becomes the belief.

The result? Adults who sabotage themselves in opposite but equally stressful ways. Some overspend because they never felt safe, so they chase safety in stuff. Others over-save because they never felt safe, so they chase safety in hoarding. Same root. Different symptom. Same anxiety.

The point isn't to blame your parents — they were just running their own scripts. The point is to notice. Because you can't rewrite a script you don't know you're following.

So ask yourself: what money messages did you grow up hearing? And more importantly: are they helping you now, or just haunting you?

Cultural Money Scripts: Scarcity, Status, and Survival

Money isn't just personal, it's cultural. The country, community, and even generation you grew up in stamped money beliefs into you long before you ever had a bank account. It's like an accent: you don't notice you have one until you talk to someone who doesn't.

Some cultures run on **scarcity scripts.** These are the "money is survival" stories. Immigrant households are a classic example. If your parents or grandparents came from poverty or political instability, you probably grew up with phrases like "save every penny," "security first," or "don't trust the system." Those lessons made sense in context — when you don't know if you'll have food next week, you learn to cling. But in adulthood, those scripts can turn into fear-driven hoarding or a constant sense of "never enough," even when you're doing fine.

Other cultures lean into **status scripts.** Here, money isn't just survival, it's proof of worth. Think "keeping up with the Joneses," but now it's Instagram flexes, designer handbags, and luxury cars you can't afford. Status scripts push you to measure success by visible markers. Doesn't matter if you're in debt, as long as the vacation photos look good. (BNPL was basically invented to turbocharge this.)

Then there are **survival scripts.** These come from environments where money is unstable — boom and bust cycles, paycheck-to-paycheck living, or communities hit hard by inequality. The message here is: spend when you have it, because who knows if it'll be there tomorrow. This explains why some people blow a tax refund in a week, not because they're "bad with money," but because culturally, money has always been fleeting. Better to enjoy it while it lasts.

And don't forget **generational scripts.**

- **Boomers** grew up with post-war stability: "Buy a house, stay loyal to your company, you'll be fine."
- **Millennials** and **Gen Z** got hit with recessions, student debt, housing crises, and pandemic chaos: "Nothing is guaranteed, the system is broken, YOLO." Same planet. Totally different money DNA.

The crazy thing is none of these scripts are "wrong." They're adaptive. They made sense in the environment they came from. But drop them into a new context, and suddenly they backfire. Scarcity culture can keep you anxious forever. Status culture can keep you broke forever. Survival culture can keep you stuck forever.

The trick isn't to erase your cultural script, it's to see it clearly. Once you know it's a script, you can decide: do I want to keep running this program, or is it time for a rewrite?

So ask yourself:

- Did you grow up in a scarcity culture that taught you safety only comes from saving?
- Did you grow up in a status culture where appearances mattered more than reality?
- Did you grow up in survival culture where money wasn't a plan, it was a fire drill?

Because you didn't invent your money beliefs. You inherited them. And until you question them, they're going to keep running the show.

The Psychology of Financial Trauma (Debt, Job Loss, Divorce)

When people hear the word *trauma*, they think car accidents, wars, terrible childhoods. They don't think unpaid credit cards or a messy divorce settlement. But here's the thing: money trauma is real trauma. It messes with your nervous system the same way. It leaves scars you can't see, but you definitely feel — every time you open your banking app and break into a cold sweat.

Think of debt. Not just owing money, but owing in a way that feels crushing, endless, humiliating. Maybe you missed payments, collectors called, interest snowballed, and suddenly your whole sense of identity shrunk down to *"I am bad with money."* Even if you've paid it off years later, you might still panic when you swipe a card, terrified it'll be declined. That's not logic. That's trauma.

Or take job loss. One day you're fine, the next day HR is handing you a box and your security is gone. For some people, that's not just a bad season — it's a before/after line. Suddenly every job feels unstable, every paycheck feels temporary, and you're living in low-key fight-or-flight mode even when things are technically okay again.

And divorce? Financial trauma dressed up in a messy breakup outfit. Splitting assets, legal bills, suddenly running a household solo — it's enough to burn financial fear into your DNA. You don't just lose a partner, you lose a sense of economic identity. Some people come out of it clutching money like oxygen. Others overspend to fill the emotional crater. Either way, the money piece lingers long after the papers are signed.

Psychology

Your nervous system wires money to safety. When money fails you, or feels like it does, your body treats it as a survival threat. Your fight/flight/freeze responses kick in. That's why:

- Some people **avoid** money completely after financial trauma (won't open bills, won't check balances).
- Others **over-control**, budgeting obsessively, terrified of any slip.
- Some swing into **over-spending**, chasing temporary relief from shame.
- Others **under-spend**, too afraid to enjoy what they have.

None of this means you're weak. It means your nervous system is doing its job: trying to keep you alive. The problem is, the danger is over, but your body hasn't gotten the memo.

And financial trauma isn't rare. According to the **APA's 2022 Stress in America survey**, nearly **65% of adults said money is a significant source of stress** in their lives. That's more than politics, health, or work. Translation: most people are walking around with some form of money trauma, whether they name it or not.

The good news? Just like other kinds of trauma, awareness is step one. Recognizing that your fear, avoidance, or compulsive behaviors come from a past wound, not from "being bad with money", is the beginning of change.

In the next section, we'll talk about breaking these patterns. Not with shame. Not by blaming your parents, culture, or ex. But by finally calling out the scripts you inherited, and deciding which ones get to stay.

Breaking Inherited Patterns Without Blame

At some point, you've probably thought: *"Thanks a lot, Mom and Dad, for screwing me up about money."* And you're not wrong. But here's the deal: blame is a dead end. It feels good for about five minutes (just like doom spending), but it doesn't fix anything.

The truth is, most of our money patterns were inherited. Parents pass down their own scripts. Cultures hand out belief systems. Trauma gets recycled. You didn't pick this starting point. But whether you keep running those scripts? That part's on you.

Think of it this way: your parents gave you a toolkit. Some of it is useful. Some of it is straight-up junk. It's like inheriting a toolbox with a rusty hammer, three broken screwdrivers, and one perfectly good wrench. You don't throw away the whole box, but you also don't keep stabbing drywall with the busted tools just because "that's what we've always used."

Examples:

- Your dad grew up in poverty and taught you to save every penny. Great, but now you're hoarding instead of investing. Time to update the script.
- Your mom treated shopping as therapy. You learned to soothe pain with purchases. Understandable, but now it's draining your paycheck. Time to rewrite the script.
- Your grandparents lived through war and drilled in "waste nothing." Useful in context. Not useful if you're rinsing and reusing paper towels like it's 1943.

Breaking patterns doesn't mean dishonoring where you came from. It means saying: *"I see why this belief existed. I get that it helped you survive. But my context is different. And I choose differently."*

This isn't about blame. Your parents weren't sitting around plotting how to ruin your financial psychology. They were just passing on the best scripts they had. Blame keeps you locked in resentment. Curiosity sets you free.

So instead of asking, *"Why did they do this to me?"* try: *"Does this belief help me today, or is it keeping me stuck?"*

That's the reset. It's not about erasing the past. It's about editing it. Keeping what serves you, ditching what doesn't, and writing new rules that match your actual life, not your grandparents' wartime ration book.

And once you start doing that? You stop repeating the history. You stop handing down the same fear, the same silence, the same status obsession to the next generation.

Which is where we're heading next: into the specific mental traps that drain your wallet daily, the biases baked into every brain that advertisers know better than you do.

Most of what we've covered so far has been about your *origin story with money*, the scripts you absorbed from family, culture, and past experiences. Those early influences explain why you react the way you do. But they're not the only forces messing with your wallet.

Because even if you grew up in a perfect household (yeah, right… no one did), your brain still comes preloaded with some pretty shady software. Cognitive biases. Mental shortcuts. The little glitches in human psychology that marketers love to exploit.

In other words: it's not just your parents or your past. Sometimes it's your own brain playing tricks on you. And in Chapter 3, we're going to drag those tricks into the light, starting with the so-called "deals" that are designed to empty your bank account.

Chapter 3:

Cognitive Biases That Empty Your Bank Account

Anchoring & Sale Traps: Why "50% Off" Isn't a Deal

Nothing lights up the human brain quite like the words **SALE.** "50% off!" "Was $299, now only $149!" Suddenly, you're not shopping, you're winning. It doesn't even matter if you actually needed the item. The deal itself feels like victory.

That's anchoring at work.

Anchoring is a psychological trick where the first number you see becomes the "anchor" your brain uses to judge value. Retailers know this, which is why they slap inflated "original prices" on everything. That $299 blender? It was *never* going to sell for $299. The anchor is fake, but your brain doesn't care, it just sees $299 and thinks $149 must be a bargain. Cue dopamine rush, cue purchase.

This is why department stores look like they're having a permanent going-out-of-business sale. It's not clearance, it's psychology.

Here's a fun fact: according to a 2022 study in the *Journal of Consumer Psychology*, simply showing a "regular price" alongside a "sale price" makes people **42% more likely** to buy, even if the sale price is just the normal price dressed up as a discount. Translation: your brain is gullible, and marketers know it.

And who among us hasn't fallen for it? You walk out of a store clutching three shirts you didn't plan to buy, muttering, *"But they were 70% off. I saved so much money."* No, you didn't save $90. You spent $30. And the shirt is still going to sit in your closet with the tag on until you donate it in two years. Congratulations, you paid $30 for clutter and a dopamine hit.

Anchoring doesn't just show up in clothing racks. It's everywhere:

- Restaurant menus put a $100 steak on the top line so the $40 steak feels "reasonable."
- Tech sites list three pricing tiers, and you magically land in the middle one, because the higher anchor made it look like the smart choice.
- Online "limited time offers" use countdown clocks to anchor urgency. (No, the sale isn't really ending in two hours. They'll reset it tomorrow. Duh…)

Anchoring works because your brain hates uncertainty. It wants a reference point. The first number it sees becomes that reference, even if it's totally arbitrary. Once it's set, your decisions orbit around it. That's why "50% off" feels like a bargain — you're anchored to the imaginary "full price," not the reality of whether you needed the damn thing in the first place.

And surprise-surprise… sales aren't designed to help you save. They're designed to **spend your future rent money today.** That's why Black Friday looks like a contact sport. It's not rational people stocking up on essentials. It's anchoring + scarcity + FOMO whipped into a frenzy.

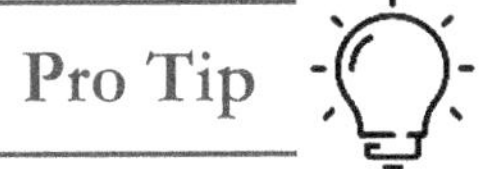

If you find yourself elbowing a stranger over a toaster, the toaster isn't the problem.

So how do you fight back? Here's the unsexy answer:

1. **Ignore the anchor.** Ask, "Would I pay this if I hadn't seen the original price?"
2. **Flip the math.** Instead of "I saved $90," reframe it as "I spent $30." Feels different, doesn't it?
3. **Check your closet.** If you already have three versions of the thing, you don't need a fourth just because it's cheap.
4. **Remember the trap.** That "original" price? Nine times out of ten, nobody ever paid it. It's fiction with a dollar sign.

Anchoring isn't going away. It's baked into every sale, every menu, every "deal of the day" email clogging your inbox. But once you spot it, you stop being the sucker. You stop mistaking "less expensive" for "worth buying."

Because a blender that was never worth $299 is still not worth $149, even if it's 50% off.

Fast Fashion & the "Free Shipping" Trap

If you've ever found yourself on Shein or Temu at 1 a.m., filling a cart with $4 shirts and kitchen gadgets you didn't know existed, you've experienced the anchoring trap in its purest form.

The pitch is always the same: *"Everything is basically free, but spend $50 to unlock free shipping."* Suddenly you're adding random crap — socks, phone cases, a glow-in-the-dark keychain, just to "save" $8 on delivery. Except now you've spent $50 you never intended to spend. That's not saving. That's math cosplay.

Fast fashion sites thrive on this illusion. They anchor you on absurdly high "original prices," then slash them by 70–90% so you feel like you're winning. But you're not buying quality pieces you'll use for years, you're stockpiling low-quality junk that falls apart after two washes. Quantity over quality. And in the long run, you're not just wasting money, you're training your brain to chase the *feeling* of deals instead of actual value.

These sites aren't accidents. They're billion-dollar labs in behavioral psychology. Every flashing banner, every countdown timer, every "other shoppers are viewing this" notice is designed to hack your brain's scarcity wiring. You don't walk away thinking *"I bought something useful."* You walk away thinking *"Wow, I scored 20 items for $50!"* until you realize you never wanted 18 of them.

And for a really sinister twist with **Temu/Shein/fast-fashion apps**: they don't just use sales psychology, they turn shopping into a *game.*

Think about it:

- **Spin-the-wheel coupons.** You "win" 100% off, which anchors you to buy *now* because it feels like a free stuff but then you need to do just a little bit more to unlock it.
- **Countdown timers.** "This deal expires in 5 minutes!" (Mhm... it won't.) That's manufactured scarcity, pushing you into panic-buy mode.
- **Points, streaks, daily check-ins.** They reward you for opening the app and "collecting coins", like it's Candy Crush, except instead of leveling up, you're training yourself to shop more.
- **Social proof pop-ups.** "1,482 people have this in their cart." Translation: FOMO as a business model.
- **Free shipping thresholds.** That classic "spend $50 to save $7" trap. It's not free shipping. It's a forced upsell disguised as generosity.

This isn't retail therapy anymore, it's casino psychology with delivery. The flashing lights, the random rewards, the "don't miss out" messaging, all of it is ripped straight from slot machine design.

And what's really crazy is people walk away not remembering *what they bought,* but remembering *how it felt to "win."* Which means they go back for another round. That's why your closet ends up stuffed with $3 shirts that looked cute online but feel like toilet paper in real life. You didn't buy value, you bought dopamine in bulk.

Case File 02

Sophie vs. the Fast-Fashion Trap

Sophie was 27, worked in marketing, and swore she didn't "really shop that much." Then she checked her phone's screen-time report: **56 minutes a night** on Shein and Temu. The apps had turned spending into a game: spin-to-win coupons, fake countdowns, and that glowing *free-shipping threshold* bar that dared her to hit $60.

Her trigger loop was a blend of *boredom + variable reward schedule,* the same psychology that keeps **slot machines** profitable. Each spin or flash sale dumped dopamine into her system, giving her a hit of excitement disguised as "rewarding myself."

We ran a micro-experiment: she **deleted both apps**, installed a **browser blocker** that forced a 10-second delay before opening any shopping site, and swapped the bedtime scroll for a 15-minute dopamine substitute: low-fi playlists and journaling her "non-purchases."

Within a month, Sophie cut **$240 in impulse buys**, shaved her screen time down by **38 minutes a night**, and said she felt "weirdly calmer, like my brain isn't buzzing for a deal anymore." The win wasn't financial, it was neurological. She'd stopped letting gamified scarcity rent space in her head.

Loss Aversion: The Fear That Keeps You Spending or Holding On

If you've ever bought something because "the sale ends tonight," even though you didn't actually need it, congrats, you've been mugged by loss aversion. If you've ever kept a subscription you don't use because "I might go back to that gym," that's loss aversion too. And if you've ever clung to a crappy investment, bad side hustle, or pair of jeans that never fit because *"I already spent the money,"* yep… same culprit.

Loss aversion is your brain's absolute obsession with avoiding loss at all costs. According to Nobel Prize–winning psychologists Daniel Kahneman and Amos Tversky, the pain of losing something is about **twice as powerful** as the pleasure of gaining it. Translation: losing $100 hurts way more than finding $100 feels good.

Marketers love this. That's why your inbox screams things like *"Don't miss out!"* or *"Only 2 left!"* They know you'll buy faster if the choice feels like preventing a loss rather than making a gain. **You're not buying the thing, you're buying protection against FOMO.**

But loss aversion doesn't just make you overspend. It makes you hold on for too long. Ever kept an old phone contract because "it's locked in"? Stayed in a streaming subscription because "what if I need it later"? Or worse, stuck with a bad financial decision just because you'd already invested time, money, or pride into it? That's the **sunk cost fallacy** — loss aversion's equally toxic cousin.

Example: you buy a $70 pair of shoes that give you blisters. A rational person would say, "These don't work, time to donate." But your brain screams, *"I paid good money for those, I can't just waste them!"* So you keep them, wear them twice more, and suffer for it. In the end, you didn't save the $70. You just added pain to the price tag.

Same goes for investments. People hang onto bad stocks because selling would "lock in the loss." So they ride the crash all the way down, clinging to the illusion of safety. Fear of losing makes them lose more.

Here's the punchline: **loss aversion makes you pay twice**. First when you spend money to avoid the "loss" of missing out. Second when you keep throwing good money (or time, or energy) after bad to avoid admitting you've already lost.

The antidote? Flip the script. Ask yourself: *"If I didn't already own this, would I buy it today?"* If the answer is no, let it go. And when it comes to "limited-time deals," remember: retailers are losing nothing when you don't buy, you are.

Loss aversion is one of the most expensive fears you'll ever carry. And until you spot it, you'll keep paying for things twice: once at the checkout, and once in regret.

Herd Mentality: FOMO, Trends, and Keeping Up with Others

Picture this: everyone on TikTok is suddenly obsessed with a Stanley Cup water bottle. You don't really need one, you already own three water bottles. But the videos make it look like the holy grail of hydration. Next thing you know, you're $60 poorer and sipping water from a cup the size of a toddler. Why? Because everyone else was doing it.

That's herd mentality in action.

Humans are pack animals. For most of history, standing out was dangerous, safety came from the group. Our brains are still wired that way. When everyone else is buying something, posting about it, or raving about it, our nervous systems go, *"Oh shit, if I don't get this, I'll be left behind."* That's why FOMO (Fear of Missing Out) is so powerful.

Marketers know this. That's why they flood you with *"best-sellers," "most popular," "trending now."* They're not just describing demand. They're manufacturing it. According to research published in the *Journal of Consumer Research*, simply labeling a product as "popular" increases sales significantly, even if no one was buying it before. Translation: crowds attract crowds.

And it's not just water bottles. Herd mentality shows up everywhere:

- **Fashion:** Shein hauls, micro-trends that die in six weeks, closets stuffed with cheap clothes you wore once.
- **Tech:** lining up overnight for the new iPhone even though your last year's one works fine.
- **Food:** $18 avocado toast, cronuts, pumpkin spice turmeric lattes.

- **Finance:** crypto bubbles, meme stocks, "hot" investments that tank as soon as the herd arrives.

The kicker is, following the herd feels safe in the moment, but it's usually expensive in the long run. By the time something is trending, it's often overpriced, overhyped, and about to flame out. You didn't miss out on a win. You dodged a stampede.

And here's the dark side: FOMO doesn't just make you spend. It makes you feel like crap about what you already have. Your perfectly fine car suddenly looks embarrassing next to your coworker's upgrade. Your vacation feels "meh" because it wasn't Bali. Your wedding feels small because Instagram told you everyone else had chandeliers and ice sculptures.

That's not budgeting, that's psychological warfare. And unless you step back, you'll keep fighting battles that don't matter, just to prove you're keeping up.

The antidote? One brutal question: *"If no one else saw this, would I still want it?"* If the answer's no, you're not buying for you. You're buying for the herd. And the herd isn't paying your bills.

Case File 03

Ravi vs. the Rocket-Emoji Economy

Ravi was a 34-year-old software engineer who'd spent most of his life being careful with money. Then came 2021, the year the internet tried to "send GameStop to the moon." His Discord chats lit up with rocket emojis, and every colleague suddenly spoke fluent meme-stock. Ravi watched friends double their accounts overnight and decided he was done being the cautious one.

He opened a trading app for the first time, threw in $8,000. His entire emergency fund. And joined the digital stampede. For two dizzying weeks his balance ballooned past $14 k. Then, just as fast, it cratered. He panic-held all the way down to $3,200.

Underneath the numbers was pure *herd behavior* and *dopamine conditioning*: validation from likes and group chats replaced rational analysis. "It wasn't even about the money," he said later. "It was about not being the idiot who missed out."

To break the cycle, Ravi built what we called a **Delay Gate** — a 48-hour cooling period before any trade, and muted every financial thread on social media. Within six months he'd recovered his savings, automated investments into index funds, and stopped waking up to market alerts. "Now," he laughed, "the only rocket emojis I like are in kids' cartoons."

Present Bias: Why "Future You" Always Gets Screwed

Here's a harsh truth: the person you screw over the most is Future You. Present You eats the cake, swipes the card, signs up for the subscription. Future You gets the cavities, the credit card bill, and the awkward call to cancel a service you forgot you had.

DEEP DIVE

Behavioral economists call this **present bias:** we overvalue immediate rewards and underweight future costs.

Studies from the Journal of Consumer Research show that "buy-now, pay-later" offers increase spending by up to **20 percent** because the pain of payment is delayed.

Label the real cost in **future-you language** ("This will cost me $X every month for Y months") to neutralize the bias.

That's present bias for you, the brain's love affair with instant gratification. We overvalue rewards we can get right now, and undervalue consequences (or rewards) that are far away.

Example: "I'll just put it on Afterpay." Present You feels relief. Future You is quietly screaming, *"I'm already juggling five other payments, what the hell are you doing?"*

Or: "Retirement? That's decades away. I'll start saving later." Present You gets the brunch. Future You gets a sad salad at 72.

This isn't laziness, it's wiring. Our brains evolved in environments where the future was uncertain. If you had food, you ate it. If you had resources, you used them. Planning for 40 years down the road? That wasn't a survival advantage when you might not survive 40 days.

But here's the modern problem: society is built on long games. Retirement savings. Mortgages. Compounding investments. And Present Bias keeps sabotaging them. According to a 2022 Vanguard report, nearly **one-third of Americans in their 40s have less than $25,000 saved for retirement.** Not because they don't know saving matters, but because Present Bias whispers, *"Later. There's always time."*

Marketers, of course, exploit this too. "Buy now, pay later." "Your first month free." "Upgrade today, deal ends tonight." They know you'll prioritize immediate pleasure over future pain. Every time you click, Present You wins, and Future You gets screwed.

Present Bias doesn't just drain your wallet. It drains your peace. Because deep down, you know you're borrowing from yourself. That nagging guilt after overspending? That's Future You glaring at you from across the timeline.

So how do you fight it? You make Future You **visible**. The more concrete the future feels, the harder it is to screw it over. That's why tools like your **Reality Dashboard** and **Future-Self Fund** (which we'll build later) are so powerful. They drag Future You into the present, so choices stop feeling abstract.

Until then, try this reframe: next time you're about to spend, imagine texting Future You. Would they reply with a thumbs up, or a middle finger? If it's the latter, maybe let it go.

We've just met the four biggest brain traps that drain your wallet: anchoring, loss aversion, herd mentality, and present bias. They're universal, sneaky, and expensive. The good news? Once you spot them, you can start hacking around them.

And that's where we're headed next: **rewiring your financial psychology** — practical tactics to outsmart your own brain and finally break free from these traps.

Bonus Content:
Money Myths That Keep You Stuck

Myth #1: "Budgeting Means No Fun"

Let's start with the myth that ruins more financial lives than TikTok shopping hauls: the belief that budgeting is basically a prison sentence for your bank account. The second people hear the word "budget," they picture a sad, joyless existence: eating plain rice, skipping every social invite, and saying, "Sorry, not in my budget" until their friends stop texting them. Somewhere along the line, budgeting got rebranded as punishment, and honestly, it's one of the most toxic money myths floating around.

But you know what? **A budget is not a diet.** Diets are all about cutting, depriving, and eventually snapping under the pressure of pretending you don't want carbs. Budgets done badly feel the same — they're all "don't spend here, don't buy that, stop wanting stuff." And like diets, those budgets almost always fail. You go through the motions for a couple weeks, feel miserable, then end up on a binge: doom spending to "reward yourself" for all the suffering. Sound familiar?

But a real budget, one that works, isn't about restriction**. It's about choice.** It's you deciding in advance what matters most and giving yourself permission to spend there without guilt. When you don't budget, every purchase feels like a micro-decision you have to justify in the moment. That's exhausting. With a budget, you've already made the decision once, so you can stop negotiating with yourself every time your phone flashes a sale notification.

Take the "fun" part. Most people assume a budget means cutting out all joy. Wrong. In fact, the smartest budgets *bake in fun money.* It might be $50 a week, it might be $200, but it's there on purpose. That means you can buy the shoes, the wine, the ridiculous Lego set... and you can do it guilt-free **because you already planned for it**. There is nothing more fun than spending money you know won't come back to bite you in the tush later.

And here's where psychology kicks in.

Psychology

Budgets actually **increase happiness** when they're designed around values. Why? Because research shows that money spent on experiences, growth, or generosity delivers more lasting joy than impulse splurges on random crap.

When your budget reflects what you actually care about, like dinners with friends, hobbies, travel, you stop bleeding money on stuff that doesn't matter and start funneling it into things that do.

Suddenly, your budget feels less like punishment and more like a custom playbook for enjoying life without financial hangovers.

Think of budgeting like GPS. Nobody complains that Google Maps is "restricting their freedom" when it tells them to turn left instead of plunging into a river. It's guidance, not a cage. A budget is the same, it keeps you on track to where you actually want to go, while still leaving plenty of room to stop for snacks along the way.

So let's kill the myth once and for all: **budgeting isn't about less fun. It's about more intentional fun.** It's the difference between buying random crap that ends up in a closet and spending on things that light you up, without guilt, without panic, and without debt collectors in your inbox.

If budgeting feels like punishment, you're doing it wrong. Done right, it feels like freedom, because it's not your impulses running the show anymore. It's you. And you've already decided fun gets a line in the budget.

Myth #2: "I'll Start Saving When I Make More Money"

This one might be the most seductive lie in personal finance. You tell yourself, *"Once I get that raise, then I'll start saving. When my side hustle picks up, that's when I'll finally build a cushion. When I'm making six figures, then I'll be serious about investing."* It sounds logical. If you have more, then you'll save more. But here's the uncomfortable truth: if you cannot save now, you probably will not save later.

Why? Because saving is not about the size of your paycheck, it is about the habit. If you spend every dollar you make at $40,000, you will spend every dollar you make at $60,000. Lifestyle creep will eat the difference before you even notice it. Suddenly, the new salary does not feel like "extra" because you've upgraded your apartment, your wardrobe, your car, your cocktails, and the restaurants you now consider "normal." It is financial quicksand disguised as progress.

There is actual research to back this up. Studies on behavioral finance consistently show that saving behavior does not automatically rise with income. In fact, many high earners are broke because their spending scales faster than their paychecks. That is why you will find people making $250,000 who are drowning in debt while their neighbor making $65,000 has a healthy savings account. It is not about the number. It is about the system.

The good news is that systems work even when the numbers are small. Saving $10 a week might sound laughable, but it is not about the ten dollars. It is about proving to yourself that you can move money out of reach before you spend it. That little move wires the habit into your brain. Later, when you do make more money, you simply increase the amount. The muscle is already built, so the upgrade feels natural instead of impossible.

Think of it like exercise. If you say, *"I'll start working out when I have more free time,"* you never will. The people who exercise consistently are not the ones with magical free calendars. They are the ones who built the habit of showing up, even for ten minutes. Same with money. Start with tiny deposits now, and scaling up later is just a matter of changing the number.

Here's a practical way to break the myth.

Pro Tip

Pick one small amount you will not miss. Maybe it is five dollars a week, maybe it is the cost of one coffee, maybe it is round-ups from your purchases. Automate it into a separate account. Label that account "Future Me." Then forget about it. Watch it grow in the background. That one action proves that saving is not about income. It is about systems.

And yes, you might argue that saving small amounts won't build wealth fast. That is true. But here's what will happen: you'll start to see the balance rise, and your brain will feel a quiet sense of pride. That pride makes you want to add more. Suddenly you are throwing in extra when you get a refund, a bonus, or just a random good day. That momentum is how the snowball starts.

So the next time you catch yourself saying, *"I'll save when I make more money,"* call it out for what it is. It is procrastination dressed up as logic. The truth is that Future You is built by Present You, one tiny deposit at a time. Waiting for "enough" is a trap, because "enough" never arrives. The habit comes first. The income just gives it more room to grow.

Myth #3: "Debt Is Always Bad"

Debt has been given the same moral weight as cheating on your spouse or kicking puppies. If you have it, you must be reckless, lazy, or doomed. Entire financial "gurus" have built empires yelling about how debt is evil and you should cut up your credit cards in some dramatic ceremony. And sure, toxic debt can be soul-sucking, but lumping all debt into one big category of "bad" is like saying all food is unhealthy because donuts exist.

Let's be clear: some debt **is** awful. High-interest credit card balances that roll month to month? Those deserve every horror story you've heard. Payday loans with triple-digit interest rates? Financial quicksand. Store cards that lure you with "special deals" and then hit you with fees when you blink? Predatory nonsense. If you're stuck in that cycle, you're basically working for your debt instead of your paycheck.

But here's where the myth falls apart: **not all debt is poison**. Some debt is leverage. A mortgage lets you own a home decades before you could pay for it in cash. Student loans, while painful, can open doors to higher earning potential. Business loans can be the bridge between a side hustle and an actual company. Even a well-managed credit card can give you benefits like fraud protection, points, or building a strong credit history. Debt itself isn't the villain, it's **how you use it**, and whether you're in control or not.

Think of debt like fire. A contained fire in your fireplace keeps you warm, cooks your food, maybe even makes the vibe a little romantic. A fire left unchecked in your living room will burn the whole house down. Same substance, different outcome.

The real trap of the "all debt is bad" myth is psychological. If you believe that carrying any debt makes you a failure, you'll hide from your statements, avoid opening emails, and feel constant shame. That shame fuels denial, and denial keeps the cycle alive. People freeze because they think the very presence of debt means they're broken. But the debt isn't the problem. The avoidance is.

A healthier way to think about it is this: debt is a tool. A hammer can build a house or smash your thumb. The difference is in how you handle it. Ask yourself three questions before deciding whether a debt is "good" or "bad":

1. Does it build long-term value (home, education, business) or just fund consumption?

2. Is the cost of borrowing (interest rate, fees) reasonable, or is it eating me alive?

3. Do I have a plan to pay it down, or am I just hoping the balance disappears by magic?

If the answers lean toward value, manageable cost, and a clear payoff plan, then that debt isn't inherently bad. It's just part of your financial toolkit. If the answers point toward high cost, no payoff plan, and nothing to show for it, then yes, that debt is a drain, and it needs tackling.

So let's retire the myth. Debt isn't a scarlet letter. It's not a personal failure stamped on your forehead. It's money you borrowed with strings attached. The goal is to learn how to manage the strings, not to live in constant fear of them.

Debt can hurt you, but it can also help you. What matters isn't whether you have it, what matters is whether you're in charge of it, or it's in charge of you.

Myth #4: "You Need Money to Make Money"

This myth has been around forever, usually delivered with a shrug by someone who has already given up: *"Well, you need money to make money."* Translation: unless you already have a trust fund, a six-figure salary, or rich parents, you might as well not bother. It sounds logical — investing a million dollars clearly generates more wealth than investing fifty bucks. But it's also a lie: you don't need piles of cash to start. Most wealth actually begins from scratch, with small, boring, repeatable moves that snowball over time.

Let's break it down. The myth has power because it contains a grain of truth. Yes, having more money gives you more options. A $10,000 investment grows faster than a $100 investment, simply because of scale. But that doesn't mean the $100 is pointless. The $100 is how you build the habit, prove to yourself you can do it, and start the compounding clock. Waiting until you have "enough" to invest is like saying you'll start working out only after you're already fit. Backwards logic.

Compounding is the magic trick here (we will cover it extensively in Chapter 9). Albert Einstein supposedly called compound interest the eighth wonder of the world. Whether he actually said it or not, the point stands: small amounts, consistently invested, grow into serious money over time. A few dollars a week in a broad index fund can turn into tens of thousands over a couple of decades. That is not theory, that's math.

Here's the psychology:

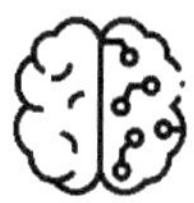

Psychology

When you tell yourself you need big money to make money, you **let yourself off the hook for starting**.

It feels safer to fantasize about what you'd do if you had a windfall than to face the reality of starting small today. That fantasy feels good. Reality feels humbling. And yet, reality is the only thing that compounds.

Real-world case studies prove this too. Look at retirement savings research. The people who end up with the largest balances aren't always the ones with the highest salaries. They're the ones who started early and stayed consistent, even with small amounts. Meanwhile, plenty of high earners hit retirement with nothing, because they assumed big income meant automatic wealth. Spoiler: it doesn't.

The other half of the myth is cultural. We love rags-to-riches stories, but what often gets skipped in the retelling are the decades of boring grind. Warren Buffett is worshipped as the ultimate money-making machine, but do you know how much of his fortune came after he turned 60? Over 90 percent. His secret isn't a genius trick. It's time, compounding, and relentless consistency.

So how do you bust this myth in your own life?

1. **Start where you are.** Even five dollars automated into savings or an investment account builds the muscle.

2. **Focus on systems, not windfalls.** Forget the fantasy of a big break. Automate tiny moves and let them stack.

3. **Value the boring.** Real wealth doesn't come from flashy hacks. It comes from quiet, predictable behaviors repeated for years.

The truth is simple: you don't need money to make money. You need habits to make money. Money just amplifies what your habits are already doing. If you build the system now, when more money does come, it has somewhere smart to go. If you don't, more money just makes the mess bigger.

So yes, rich people have an advantage. But the starting line is available to everyone. And the people who win aren't the ones who wait for a head start. They're the ones who start running with what they've got.

Myth #5: "Lots of Money Will Make Me Happy"

This one is sneaky, because it sounds obvious. Of course, money makes life easier. Of course, it is better to have it than not. But somewhere between "money helps" and "money guarantees happiness," the wires get crossed. And that's where people chase their whole lives trying to hit some magic number, only to realize it doesn't work the way they thought.

Happiness doesn't live in your bank account. **It lives in your head**. Right now, maybe you feel unhappy because you can't afford the new TV. Meanwhile, a millionaire feels unhappy because they can't afford a villa on Lake Como. **Same feeling, different price tag.** Money just upgrades the set design of your unhappiness. It doesn't remove it.

Psychologists call this the **hedonic treadmill.** Every time you level up financially, your expectations level up too. You get a raise, you feel great for about five minutes, then suddenly the car you loved looks shabby compared to your coworker's upgrade. You move into a bigger place, and within a year you're scrolling real estate listings again, convinced you need even more space. It never ends, because your brain is wired to adapt. What felt like abundance yesterday feels like "not enough" tomorrow.

There is research here too. According to studies from Princeton (Kahneman & Deaton, 2010), happiness does rise with income, but only up to a point. In the U.S., that number was around $75,000 a year (adjusted for inflation, call it closer to $100,000 now). Beyond that, more money keeps increasing your sense of "life satisfaction," but it does not make you happier day to day. Translation: **more money means fewer financial problems, but it doesn't fix emotional ones.**

That's why you see miserable millionaires and surprisingly content people on modest incomes. Once your basics are covered — food, shelter, safety, the ability to say yes to some fun, happiness stops being about the size of your wallet and starts being about how you spend your time, who you spend it with, and how you think about what you already have.

And here's what's interesting: chasing money as the main source of happiness usually **backfires**. The more you tie your mood to dollars, the more fragile your mood becomes. Stocks dip, mood dips. Job gets shaky, mood collapses. You hand over control of your emotional state to forces you cannot control. That is a terrible trade.

So what's the reframe? Money is not happiness. Money is **a tool that buys options.** Options to say no to work you hate, to take time off, to support people you love, to design a life that fits you. That freedom can create happiness if you use it intentionally. But the money itself? It is just numbers. If you don't work on your mindset, those numbers will never be enough.

Lots of money won't make you happy. But using whatever money you have to build calm, freedom, and meaningful choices? That just might.

Myth #6: "If I Just Work Hard Enough, I'll Be Rich"

This myth is baked deep into our culture. It's the backbone of every "American Dream" speech, every motivational hustle post, every corporate pep talk that tells you to "go the extra mile." The story goes like this: if you work hard, keep your head down, and grind longer than everyone else, wealth will eventually show up at your doorstep like an Amazon delivery. Sounds noble. Also sounds exhausting. Unfortunately, it's not how money actually works.

Don't get me wrong: hard work matters. If you refuse to show up, you won't build anything. But equating hard work with automatic wealth is a trap. Plenty of people bust their asses at two jobs, pull overtime, and still live paycheck to paycheck. Nurses, teachers, tradies, hospitality workers — some of the hardest working people you'll ever meet, often struggle financially, not because they're lazy, but because the system doesn't pay them in proportion to their effort. Meanwhile, you've probably met people coasting in cushy jobs, raking in way more for half the grind. The difference isn't effort. It's leverage.

Here's the real equation: **wealth = value × leverage × consistency.** Hard work is in there, sure, but it's just one factor. If all you do is trade hours for dollars, your income is capped by time and energy. There are only so many hours you can physically grind. At some point, you burn out. Leverage is what breaks the ceiling — things like skills, assets, systems, and investments that keep working when you're asleep.

Take investing. You could work 80 hours a week at minimum wage and never get ahead. But $100 invested monthly in an index fund compounds without you breaking a sweat. That's leverage. Or take automation, setting up savings and bills to run in the background. That's your money system working while you're busy living, not another shift at work.

The myth of "hard work equals wealth" is also dangerous because it **keeps people quiet**. It tells you if you're struggling, it's your fault for not grinding hard enough. That shame shuts down real conversations about wages, financial literacy, or systemic inequality. It tricks people into thinking the solution is just more sweat, when the truth is sweat without strategy won't get you anywhere.

So, the reframe is: **hard work is fuel, not the engine**. If you pour fuel into a broken car, you don't get anywhere faster. But if the engine is built well with systems, habits, and assets, then even a modest amount of fuel takes you far. The goal is not to grind endlessly, it is to work hard *once* to set up systems that work hard forever.

So how do you break this myth in your own life?

1. **Stop measuring only in hours.** Ask, "How can I make my effort compound?"
2. **Invest in skills**. New knowledge and abilities multiply the value of your work.
3. **Automate and systemize.** Build processes that run without your constant energy.
4. **Use money to buy freedom, not just stuff.** Wealth isn't about working harder; it's about buying back time.

So, the saddest part is: you can grind yourself into dust and still not build wealth. Hard work matters, but it's not the whole story. Smart systems, leverage, and consistency are what turn effort into freedom.

Hustle without strategy is just exhaustion. Hustle with systems? That's how you build wealth without breaking yourself.

Case Study: When Money Isn't the Solution

When we say money is a tool, not freedom, this story proves exactly why we mean it.

Jack Whittaker was already doing well—he ran a construction business in West Virginia—when he hit a $314 million Powerball jackpot in December 2002. After taxes he walked away with roughly $113 million in cash. That could've been whole-lifetime security. What came next is a cautionary manual on money without mindset.

Almost immediately, he became a walking ATM. He drove around in a Lamborghini, handed out houses to convenience store clerks, and pledged millions to local churches. But the celebration didn't last. Thieves broke into his car twice, stealing hundreds of thousands in cash he literally carried around. One thief even tried lacing his drink with drugs before robbing him. The worst came when his granddaughter's boyfriend was found dead in his home—thanks, in part, to the toxicity money can expose.

In a few short years, Jack's fortunes reversed. He was embroiled in legal disputes, lost control of money, and his personal life unraveled. When he died in 2020, he was no longer the Powerball legend, just a man who had lost himself to the chaos his wealth created.

But Jack's isn't the only tragic case. **Collin McLeod**, a modest lottery winner from Ontario, won $1 million in 2018. He had a stable job, some inheritance, and a life that felt within control. Yet, within years he was flat broke, down to just $97, suffering from health issues, legal trouble, even loss of personal possessions… and his own father's ashes had been stolen. "I wish I never won," he later said.

Both stories share a powerful truth: **money magnifies what's inside of us**. Without emotional boundaries, systems, and identity, it can destroy you.

So what does that look like if you want a different ending?

- You build systems first. Debt-free defaults, savings, dashboards, so a windfall doesn't become a whirlwind.
- You create emotional structures. Boundaries, accountability, professional advice.
- You anchor identity. Jack and Collin were rich overnight. But without an identity as "calm, wise steward," that money became a curse, not freedom.

These stories aren't the norm, but they matter. They remind us: money does not fix your story. You have to write a system and identity that can handle what might come through the door—planned or not.

PART II:

Rewiring Your Financial Psychology

Chapter 4:

Interrupting the Urge

(Impulse Spending Tactics That Work)

The 10-Second Pause: Training Your "Stop" Muscle

Impulse spending is like muscle memory. You see it, you want it, you buy it, often before your brain has even caught up. Your finger hits *"Add to Cart"* faster than your common sense can get a word in.

The antidote? Build a *stop muscle.* And the simplest way to do that is the **10-Second Pause.**

Here's how it works: When you feel the urge to buy something online, in-store, anywhere… you stop. You literally pause. Ten slow seconds. That's it. No buying, no tapping, no clicking. Just wait.

Why does this matter? Because those ten seconds buy you a slice of awareness. Most impulses fade as fast as they appear. Give your brain a gap, and you can actually ask yourself questions like:

- *Do I actually need this?*
- *Do I already own something that does the same job?*
- *Would I still want this tomorrow?*
- *Is this about the item, or about my mood?*

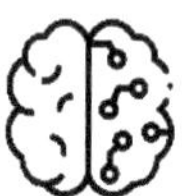

Psychology

When you pause, you're **shifting control** from your limbic system (the impulsive, emotional part of your brain) to your prefrontal cortex (the logical, decision-making part). It's like hitting the brakes before you drive off a cliff. Nine times out of ten, the urge shrinks once you shine a light on it.

And yes, ten seconds sounds ridiculously small, but that's the point. You don't need heroic willpower. You just need a crack in the automatic loop.

Example**:** You're doom-scrolling at 11 p.m. Temu flashes you a "90% off, ending soon!" deal on a desk lamp shaped like a cat. Your finger twitches. Instead of clicking, you stop. Ten seconds. In that gap, your brain goes: *"Wait. I already have two lamps. This isn't about lighting. This is about boredom."* You close the app. Congratulations, Future You just dodged $25 of regret.

Pro Tip

If ten seconds feels too easy, level it up. Try the **10-10-10 Rule:** pause 10 seconds, then ask — how will I feel about this purchase in 10 minutes? 10 days? 10 months? That fast-forwards you past the dopamine hit into the regret phase. If it looks dumb in ten months, it's probably dumb now.

Impulse Buy | **Paused Decision**

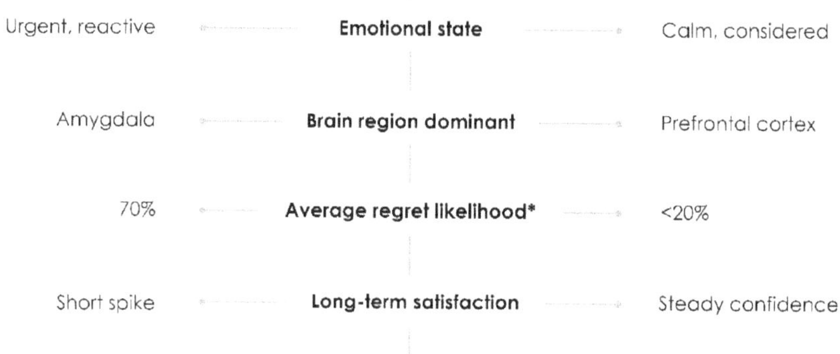

**Percentages from behavioral-economics studies on delayed gratification (Stanford, 2020).*

A short pause rewires the decision from emotional to logical. Each second adds control.

Will the pause stop *every* impulse buy? Nope. Sometimes you'll still go for it. (And hey, sometimes that's okay.) The goal isn't to eliminate spending. It's to **break the reflex**. To remind yourself that buying isn't the only option.

The more you practice the pause, the stronger your stop muscle gets. Eventually, it becomes your second nature. Your hand hovers over the button, your brain whispers *"pause,"* and boom!.. you're back in control.

Think of it like financial push-ups. Each pause is a rep. Small on its own. Transformative when stacked.

Cart Quarantine: The 24-Hour Rule That Saves Hundreds

Impulse spending thrives on immediacy. The cart is full, the button is glowing, your brain is whispering *"Do it, you deserve it."* And before you know it, the package is on its way.

The cure? Put your cart in quarantine.

Here's the rule: When you want to buy something that isn't a genuine necessity, you add it to your cart… and leave it there for 24 hours. No exceptions. No checkout. Just let it sit.

Why it works:

- **Dopamine fade.** That shopping high loses its power when you delay. What felt urgent yesterday often feels irrelevant today.
- **Clarity check.** You get space to ask: *Do I still want this, or was I just in a mood?*
- **Budget honesty.** Waiting forces you to consider how the purchase fits into your actual money plan, not just your feelings.

Most people are shocked by how many "must-haves" turn into *"eh, never mind"* after a day. According to a 2021 LendingTree survey, more than **60% of Americans admitted to regretting impulse purchases,** and nearly half said waiting even 24 hours would've saved them money.

Example: You see a $90 pair of sneakers online. They look amazing. You're convinced they'll change your life. You add them to your cart… and wait. Next day, you open the cart and realize you already have three pairs of sneakers. Suddenly, the $90 feels less like destiny and more like clutter. Delete. Money saved.

But here's the magic twist: sometimes after 24 hours, you *still* want the thing. And that's okay. The rule isn't "never buy." It's "don't buy without giving your brain a chance to catch up." If it passes the quarantine test, buy it guilt-free.

This isn't just about online shopping, either. In stores, try a "mental cart." Hold the item. Walk around for ten minutes. If you still want it, fine. If you forget about it, even better. (reality is: most people forget.)

The Cart Quarantine isn't glamorous. It's not a spreadsheet or a fancy app. But it works, because it hacks the core problem: urgency. Retailers want you to believe that buying now = happiness. Quarantine teaches you that waiting = freedom.

So next time you're hovering over "Place Order," remember: your cart isn't a checkout line. It's a waiting room. Let the item sit there. If it's worth buying, it'll survive the night.

The "Wishlist Wednesday" Technique for Delayed Gratification

Impulse buying is sneaky because it feels urgent: *"If I don't get this right now, I'll die."* (I swear, you won't.) The problem isn't that you want things. It's that you want them **immediately.** Enter: **Wishlist Wednesday.**

Here's the trick: instead of buying something the moment you want it, you add it to a master wishlist. Then, and only then, you review that list once a week, on Wednesdays.

Why Wednesday? Because it's random enough not to overlap with your typical high-temptation days (payday weekends, late-night boredom, Sunday "treat yourself" vibes). By the time Wednesday rolls around, two things usually happen:

1. Half the stuff on the list has lost its appeal.
2. The things still calling your name are actual wants, not fleeting impulses.

Example: On Friday, you see a $30 gadget on TikTok that promises to slice avocado six ways. You want it. You add it to your wishlist. By Wednesday, you look at the list and think, *"Why the hell would I ever need that?"* Delete. Money saved.

But maybe one item sticks. A book you've wanted for weeks. A jacket you'll wear all winter. By waiting, you separate impulse from intention. That's delayed gratification in action, and it feels even better than the instant high, because now you're buying with clarity instead of chaos.

This isn't just psychology fluff, it's **behavioral science**. Delayed gratification is one of the most reliable predictors of financial success. Remember the famous "marshmallow test," where kids who waited for two marshmallows instead of grabbing one immediately ended up more successful later in life? Wishlist Wednesday is your grown-up marshmallow test. Except with fewer sticky fingers and cleaner credit card statements.

Pro Tip

Make your wishlist visible. Keep it in your phone notes, a budgeting app, or even a whiteboard at home. The act of writing it down gives you the dopamine hit of *"I've acknowledged my want"* without actually spending. Half the satisfaction, zero the cost.

And the best part? Reviewing your list can become a mini ritual. Coffee in hand, scrolling through your past "urgent" desires, laughing at how dumb half of them look now. It's like a highlight reel of things you didn't waste money on. Future You will thank Present You for this one.

Substituting Dopamine: Healthy Alternatives to Retail Therapy

Our problem is: retail therapy works. Swiping, clicking, unboxing, it's a dopamine buffet. The problem with our problem isn't that shopping makes you feel good. It's that it makes you feel good **briefly,** then dumps you into regret, debt, and shame.

So here's the hack: don't kill the dopamine. **Replace it.**

Your brain doesn't actually care *where* the dopamine comes from. It just wants a hit. Which means if you can swap the "buy now" trigger for something else that gives you the same chemical buzz, you get the relief *without* the receipt.

Here are some swaps that work:

- **The 5-Minute Walk Hit.** Step outside. Move your body. Your brain gets endorphins, your nervous system calms, and you don't end up with another pair of sweatpants.
- **The Text-a-Friend Trick.** Connection spikes dopamine, too. Instead of opening Temu, open your messages. Tell a friend something dumb or funny. Cheaper and more rewarding.
- **The Playlist Reset.** Blast one high-energy song. Dance like a fool in your kitchen. Boom — dopamine, zero dollars.
- **Micro-Cleaning.** Weirdly effective. Wipe your counters, fold laundry, or make your bed. Your brain loves completion, and suddenly you've swapped "checkout complete" for "task complete."

- **The Cheap-but-Cheerful List.** If spending feels unavoidable, make a list of under-$5 pleasures (coffee, fancy soap, a plant cutting). Use those as your "safe hits" instead of $200 impulse buys.

This isn't about denying yourself joy. It's about upgrading your coping mechanism. Because shopping for comfort is like eating candy for dinner: it works in the moment, but it wrecks you long-term. Dopamine swaps let you get the buzz *and* keep your money.

And no, this doesn't mean you'll never shop again. It just means shopping won't be your only lever when life feels heavy. You'll have a menu of other options that give your brain the same reward without the debt hangover.

Pro Tip

Track your swaps. Every time you redirect an urge, jot it down. Watching that list grow becomes its own dopamine hit. ("Look at me, dodging purchases like a ninja.")

And here's the even bigger truth: money management isn't just about numbers. It's about managing emotions. If you don't replace retail therapy with something else that feels good, you'll keep running back to the checkout line. Substitution isn't optional. It's survival.

In a nutshell, impulse spending isn't a character flaw. It's a brain pattern. But once you start training the stop muscle, quarantining carts, delaying gratification, and swapping dopamine sources, the pattern breaks.

Next up: we'll make your environment do half the work for you. Chapter 5 is about setting up systems — friction, defaults, and little tricks that make good money choices automatic and bad ones annoying.

Chapter 5:

Friction & Defaults: How to Outsmart Yourself with Systems

Automating Bills & Savings to Bypass Willpower

Here's the thing about willpower: it's unreliable as hell. It shows up strong in the morning when you're caffeinated and motivated, and then it disappears the second life throws something at you — a fight with your boss, a bad sleep, a stressful bill you weren't expecting. If your whole financial plan is built on *"I'll be disciplined every month,"* then honestly, you're already setting yourself up to fail, because discipline is basically the flimsiest building material you could use.

The real secret isn't trying harder. It's **removing the need to try** at all. And that's where automation comes in.

Automation is like brushing your teeth. You don't wake up every morning, stare into the mirror, and negotiate with yourself about whether or not to brush, you just do it, because it's automatic, because it's a habit you don't have to think about. When you set your money up the same way, you're not relying on your future tired, emotional, over-stimulated self to "make the right choice." You're outsourcing that choice to a system that doesn't get stressed or bored or tempted by a TikTok haul video at 11 p.m.

Start with bills. Because nothing kills financial calm faster than missing a payment and suddenly you've got late fees, angry letters, and the creeping sense that you're terrible at this whole being an adult nonsense. Automating your bills means that even if you're having the worst week of your life, your rent still gets paid, your lights stay on, and your credit score doesn't get quietly murdered in the background. Does it hurt a little when the money just leaves your account automatically? Sure. But it hurts way less than forgetting, scrambling, and then paying an extra $60 for the privilege of being disorganized.

And then there's the magic piece: **savings**. Most people think, *"I'll just save whatever's left at the end of the month."* And you already know how that story ends, nothing is left. Because you'll always find something to spend it on. Future You doesn't get the leftovers; they get nothing. So you have to flip it. Automate your savings the same way you automate Netflix. Set up a transfer that skims money off the top of your paycheck before you even see it, before your brain has a chance to argue about how much you "need" to keep in checking. Out of sight, out of temptation.

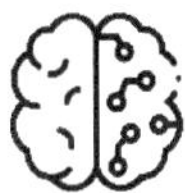

Psychology

Researchers call this the **default effect**. Humans are wired to stick with whatever the default is. If you have to manually decide to move money into savings every month, you won't. But if it's the default, if it happens automatically, you won't fight it. You'll just accept it as normal. That's why this works even if you're only saving $20 at first. It's not the amount that matters; it's the muscle memory you're building.

And don't just automate the "boring" responsible stuff. **You can automate the fun, too.** Create a guilt-free spending account, set up a little transfer every payday, and then when you want to splurge, you're pulling from a pot that was literally built for joy. That way you're not raiding rent money for your Friday night cocktails, and you can actually enjoy yourself without the side order of guilt.

This isn't just me ranting about theory. The **Commonwealth Bank of Australia** found in 2023 that people who set up automatic transfers into savings accounts ended up with balances about **60% higher after a year** compared to people who tried to move money manually. Not because they earned more, not because they were smarter, just because they got out of their own damn way.

That's the whole point: automation is financial autopilot. It bypasses your flaky willpower, skips the guilt spiral, and builds wealth in the background while you're busy living your life. You don't have to feel motivated every day. You don't even have to think about it. You just set it up once, and the system does the heavy lifting while you do literally anything else.

Discipline is overrated. Defaults win every time.

Setting "Friction Walls" Between You and Your Weak Spots

Most people think the way to get better with money is to have more discipline, but who are we kidding: discipline is a terrible long-term strategy. It's like trying to run a marathon fueled entirely by espresso shots, sure, you'll make it through the first stretch, but eventually you'll crash. What works better than discipline is design. Specifically, designing your environment so dumb money decisions become harder, and smart money decisions become easier. That's what I call **friction walls**.

Here's the deal: spending has been engineered to be frictionless. Amazon, Temu, Shein, PayPal, Afterpay — they've all spent billions making sure you can go from "I want it" to "It's on the way" in under thirty seconds. Your brain barely has time to blink before your bank account has already been looted. Which means if you want to stop blowing money on things you don't even remember buying, you've got to throw some speed bumps back into the process.

That might mean deleting your saved card info so you actually have to get off the couch, grab your wallet, and type in those sixteen digits every time you want something. Or logging out of shopping apps so you can't just open them and scroll half-asleep while you're watching Netflix. Or unsubscribing from those "flash sale" emails that exist for one reason only: to bypass your brain and push your thumb straight to *Buy Now.*

And this isn't just theory. Let me tell you about Ella. She wrote on her blog (*The Tidy Leaf*) that she was drowning in impulse purchases — little gadgets, home knick-knacks, random late-night "treats." Nothing massive on its own, but it added up. Her weak spot was PayPal's one-click checkout. Every time she wanted something, it was a two-second transaction. No pause, no thought, no friction. So she decided to delete PayPal from her phone. That's it. One tiny, annoying change. And it completely rewired her spending.

Suddenly, every time she wanted to buy something, she had to go grab her laptop, log in, and manually put in her card details. And you know what? Nine times out of ten, she couldn't be bothered. That little wall between her and her impulses saved her hundreds of dollars. She started noticing what she actually wanted versus what she just "wanted right now." And once the overspending slowed down, she had room to start saving intentionally.

That's the power of friction. It doesn't require you to be a saint. It just forces you to **think long enough for your logical brain to catch up.**

And here's the beautiful twist for you: you can do the opposite with good habits. Remove friction from the stuff you *want* to do more of. Make saving automatic so it happens without thought. Use an app that rounds up your purchases into investments so you're building wealth with zero effort. Put a budgeting tracker on your home screen so logging an expense is two taps instead of twenty.

Because humans are lazy. We follow the path of least resistance. If you make bad habits harder and good habits easier, you don't have to fight yourself anymore. You just let your environment do the heavy lifting.

Challenge

Think about the last **three dumb things you bought**. Now ask: if there had been even one extra step in the way, entering your card, finding your password, walking to your laptop, would you still have gone through with it? If the answer is no, then you've just identified your first friction wall. Build it.

Because at the end of the day, it's not about having iron willpower. It's about outsmarting the companies that are trying to strip all the friction out of spending. Put the walls back in place, and suddenly you're not at their mercy anymore.

Environment Design: Making Overspending Hard and Saving Easy

You don't rise to the level of your intentions, you sink to the level of your environment. Which means if your world is set up to push you into bad money habits, you will eventually fall into them no matter how strong your willpower is. The flip side is also true: if your world is arranged to make good money choices stupidly easy, you'll fall into those instead.

That's environment design. Unlike walls to block temptation we just talked about, this is **offense,** rigging the field so your laziest, most distracted self still stumbles into better choices.

Think about it like this: supermarkets put candy at the checkout for a reason. They know you're tired, you're over it, and you'll grab something without thinking. That's environment design. They didn't add friction; they smoothed the path. Your job is to flip that logic and design your environment so the easy grab is the one that helps you.

Here's what it looks like in practice:

- **Make saving automatic and visible.** Put a "Future You" account right at the top of your banking app so you see it every time you log in. Watching the number grow is addictive. It becomes the candy at the checkout, except this candy is compounding quietly in your favor.
- **Keep a money tracker in plain sight.** A sticky note on your fridge with your weekly budget. A whiteboard near your desk showing progress on a savings goal. Humans love visible reminders. You're tricking your brain into chasing the green ticks instead of chasing the next "add to cart."

- **Engineer your kitchen and workspace.** If you always overspend on Uber Eats, make home cooking the path of least resistance: pre-chop veggies, keep quick meals on hand, leave your pan on the stove so the barrier to cooking is tiny. If you're tempted by takeout coffee, set your mug by the door at night and your beans in the grinder so making coffee is easier than detouring to Starbucks.
- **Use tech against itself.** Move your budgeting app to your home screen. Turn on bank alerts for big transactions. Set your savings app to send you dopamine-pinging notifications when you hit milestones.

Notice how this is different from friction walls. Friction walls are about *slowing down bad behavior*. Environment design is about *speeding up good behavior*. It's not just protection, it's proactive manipulation — of yourself, by yourself.

And here's the best part: you only have to design the system once, but it pays off every day. You don't have to "decide" to be good with money a hundred times a week, your environment decides for you. Your fridge layout, your phone apps, your banking setup, they do the nudging so you don't have to fight.

Because whilst your willpower is temporary, environments are permanent. And the people who win with money aren't necessarily stronger, smarter, or luckier. They're just playing on a field that's tilted in their favor.

The One-Click Rule: Creating Mental Speed Bumps

We live in a world where you can buy almost anything with one click. And that's the problem. Because when the gap between *wanting* something and *owning* it is about two seconds, your brain doesn't stand a chance.

That's where the **One-Click Rule** comes in. It's simple: if buying something takes less than one click, you're in danger. So you deliberately build in extra clicks, little speed bumps, to slow the process down.

Think of it like this: imagine if every online purchase required you to do ten push-ups first. How much less random crap would you own right now? That's the principle, except you don't actually need to get sweaty, you just need digital speed bumps.

Here are a few:

- **Delete your stored cards.** If your payment info is saved on Amazon or PayPal, erase it. Now you actually have to get up, fetch your wallet, and type it in like it's 2005. By the time you've dug under the couch cushions looking for your card, the "must-have" purchase probably won't feel so urgent anymore.
- **Turn off one-click checkout.** Amazon literally patented the one-click purchase button to bypass your brain. Go into settings and disable it. If you can't, add friction manually (different password, no autofill, logout after each session).
- **Add a "reason step."** Before buying, force yourself to type one sentence into your phone notes: *"I'm buying this because…"* That 10-second pause forces your prefrontal cortex online.

Half the time, you'll cringe at your own excuse and close the tab.

- **Use two-device confirmation.** For bigger purchases, make it a rule that you can only check out on your laptop, not your phone. That tiny extra step, putting your phone down, walking to your computer, is enough to kill most impulses.

And believe me: speed bumps won't feel like punishment once they're in place. At first you'll groan when you have to re-enter your card number. But after a while, you'll realize the number of pointless purchases tanked, your bank account looks calmer, and the stuff you *do* buy actually feels intentional.

Remember: retailers spend billions trying to remove every single click between you and "Buy Now." Your job is to add some back. Because the difference between one click and three clicks might not sound like much, but it's the exact gap where common sense has room to wake up.

So the rule is simple: **if it only takes one click, make it take three.** Future You will thank you for every extra speed bump you install.

We've just spent several chapters hacking the hardware of your money life: automating bills, setting up friction walls, rearranging your environment, and dropping speed bumps into your checkout flows. All of that matters because it takes willpower out of the equation and makes good decisions easier than bad ones.

But systems alone don't solve the whole problem. Because if you've ever felt your chest tighten opening a bank app, or avoided looking at your credit card balance like it was a horror movie, you already know money isn't just numbers, it's feelings. Anxiety, shame, panic, even guilt.

And those feelings don't just make you miserable. They drive your behavior. They're why you overspend, avoid, or spiral. Which means the next step isn't more hacks, it's learning how to deal with the emotional weight of money.

So in Chapter 6, we're switching gears. We're going to build **emotional safety nets** — tools that help you stay calm, present, and clear-headed when money stress hits, so you can make decisions without fear running the show.

Chapter 6:

Emotional Safety Nets: Building Calm Around Money

Reframing Financial Anxiety as a Signal, Not a Threat

Money anxiety is universal. You are not broken if your chest tightens before you open your banking app. You are human. In fact, money is the number one reported source of stress in the U.S., according to the **American Psychological Association's 2022 Stress in America survey**. That means if you are sweating when you swipe your card, you are in good company. Two out of three people feel the same way.

Here is the reframe: anxiety itself is not the problem. The problem is how we interpret it. Most of us treat financial anxiety like a threat, as if the worry itself is proof we are failing. So we numb it with spending, avoid it by ignoring our bills, or spiral into shame.

What if instead you treated financial anxiety as a signal? Think of it like a dashboard light in your car. The light is not the engine exploding. It is simply information: *"Something needs attention here."*

Some examples:

- If your anxiety spikes every time you look at your credit card balance, the signal might be that you need a clearer system for managing debt.
- If you panic when you think about retirement, the signal might be that you have not built a simple plan for Future You yet.
- If your heart races every time rent comes out, the signal might be that your buffer is too thin and you need a small cushion.

The feeling itself is not failure. It is your body trying to get your attention.

And here is the truth: ignoring money anxiety does not make it disappear. It makes it louder. Just like ignoring that dashboard light until the engine starts smoking. The longer you avoid, the scarier it feels, and the more dramatic the fixes have to be. But when you see it as a signal, you can respond instead of react.

A therapist once described anxiety as "your brain running fire drills to keep you safe." It is clumsy, often misfired, and sometimes loud as hell, but it is not out to destroy you. Your job is to separate the useful signals from the false alarms.

So the next time your stomach flips before checking your bank account, do not tell yourself *"I am bad with money."* Try this instead:

1. Pause.
2. Label the feeling: *"This is anxiety, not danger."*
3. Ask: *"What is this anxiety pointing to? What small step could make this feel less threatening?"*

Maybe it is creating a one-page dashboard so you are not juggling ten accounts in your head. Maybe it is setting up one automatic savings transfer so you feel less unprotected. Maybe it is just logging in once a week instead of once a month so the numbers stop feeling like a horror reveal.

The point is simple. Financial anxiety is trying to talk to you. If you treat it as a signal, you can listen, adjust, and move forward. If you treat it as a threat, you will keep dodging it until it burns you.

This is why the next step is building tools that quiet the panic in real time. It is not enough to just reframe the anxiety. You also need a practical way to see your money clearly without triggering fight-or-flight. That is where your long promised **Reality Dashboard** comes in.

The Reality Dashboard: One-Page Snapshot That Quiets Panic

One of the biggest drivers of money stress is not actually the money itself, it is the fog. You know the feeling. You sort of know what is in your account, you vaguely know what bills are coming, you have a rough idea of how much debt is sitting there, but the numbers never line up in your head. It is like trying to drive through a storm with the windshield covered in mud. No wonder you are anxious.

The cure is not spreadsheets with fifty tabs. The cure is a one-page snapshot that shows you exactly where you stand. I call it the **Reality Dashboard**.

Here is the idea: everything important lives on one page. Not ten apps, not three different notebooks, not a mental list that falls apart the second you get distracted. Just a clear snapshot of the numbers that actually matter.

What goes on it?

- **Current balances.** Checking, savings, and credit cards. No hiding.
- **Monthly essentials.** Rent or mortgage, utilities, groceries, transport.
- **Recurring extras.** Subscriptions, memberships, or anything sneaky that drains your account while you are not looking.
- **Debt snapshot.** Total owed, interest rates, and minimums.
- **Savings and future funds.** Emergency fund, retirement, or even just a small account for Future You.

That is it. One page. Enough to orient you without sending you into Excel-induced despair.

Why does this work? Because **anxiety feeds on vagueness**. Your brain hates uncertainty, so when you have no idea what the real picture looks like, it fills in the blanks with worst-case scenarios. That is why your balance feels terrifying before you log in, but once you actually see the number, it is rarely as bad as your imagination made it.

The dashboard also **shifts your relationship with money**. Instead of treating it like a monster lurking in the dark, you are turning the light on. The monster shrinks. Suddenly you can see where things are leaking, where you are actually fine, and where a small change would make a big difference.

And yes, the first time you set it up might sting. Nobody likes looking at their numbers straight on. But here is the surprising part: after the initial sting comes calm. Because now you know. And knowing gives you control.

I had a friend who avoided her credit card statement for months. She was convinced it was catastrophic, like "ruin my life forever" catastrophic. When she finally faced it and put the number on her dashboard, it was about half what she had imagined. Still serious, but no longer the monster in the closet. She could see it, plan for it, and chip away at it. That is the power of clarity.

The dashboard does not need to be fancy. A notebook page. A whiteboard. A simple Google Sheet. Even the Notes app on your phone. The format is irrelevant. The point is that it exists, it is one page, and you look at it regularly.

Over time, the dashboard stops being a source of dread and becomes a source of reassurance. You open it and think, "Okay, here is what is true. Here is what I need to do." No fog, no monsters, no guessing games.

Once you have the Reality Dashboard in place, you finally have the clarity to experiment. And that is the next step: creating **safe-to-fail experiments with money**. Instead of treating every choice like a life-or-death test, you set up small experiments where mistakes are allowed and learning is the goal. That is how you build real confidence with money.

Creating Safe-to-Fail Experiments With Money

Most of us treat money decisions like they are life-or-death trials. Every choice feels loaded: if you screw this up, you are doomed forever. Which is why so many people freeze, avoid, or spend half their lives Googling "best savings account" without ever opening one.

Most money decisions are not permanent, they are experiments. And the best way to lower your anxiety is to design them as safe-to-fail experiments.

A safe-to-fail experiment is exactly what it sounds like. You set up a small, low-stakes test that lets you learn without blowing yourself up if it goes sideways.

Examples:

- Instead of overhauling your entire budget, try tracking spending for one week and see what happens.
- Instead of deciding whether investing is "for you" once and for all, put $20 into a simple index fund and watch how it feels.
- Instead of swearing off Uber Eats forever, set a two-week limit of twice per week and see if you actually feel happier with that boundary.

The point is not to get it perfect. The point is to gather data about how you behave and how it feels.

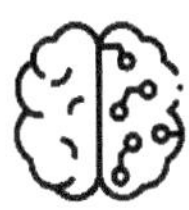

Psychology

Why this works: you feel most anxious when things are ambiguous. When the stakes feel huge, your nervous system goes into overdrive. Safe-to-fail experiments shrink the stakes. They turn "I have to get this right or I am screwed" into "let me try this small thing and see what I learn." That shift pulls you out of paralysis and back into action.

And yes, you will sometimes "fail." You will set a budget and blow it. You will invest in something that dips right after you buy. You will try to cook at home and end up ordering pizza anyway. That's fine. **Failure is the point**. You are learning what works for you, what feels good, and what habits are actually sustainable instead of theoretical.

I once spoke with a guy who was terrified of investing. He had read a hundred blogs, watched hours of YouTube, and convinced himself that if he picked the wrong option, he would ruin his future. He finally agreed to try a safe-to-fail experiment: he invested $50 into a boring index fund. Two weeks later, nothing catastrophic had happened. The world had not ended. The number in his account had wiggled up and down a little, and suddenly investing felt less like gambling and more like math. That one tiny experiment unlocked him to start building a habit.

The psychology here is simple. Humans learn by doing, not by overthinking. Safe-to-fail experiments give you permission to act, which is the only way confidence grows. You do not wait until you feel confident to try something. You try something small, and the confidence follows.

Challenge

Pick one money area that **stresses you out** and design a **safe-to-fail experiment**. Keep the stakes tiny, keep the time frame short, and write down what you learn. Do not judge the result as "success" or "failure." Judge it by whether you got useful information you can build on.

That is how financial calm is built: not through one perfect plan, but through dozens of messy little experiments that teach you how you work.

And while experiments reduce anxiety, there is one more piece most people miss. You cannot beat yourself up every time you stumble. **Self-compassion** is not fluff here. It is a financial strategy, because shame drains your energy faster than any bad purchase.

Self-Compassion as a Financial Strategy

Here is something you almost never hear in the world of money advice: being kind to yourself is not fluffy self-care, it is a financial tactic. And it might be the one thing standing between you and actual progress.

Because shame is expensive. Think about it. Every time you beat yourself up for overspending, or spiral after looking at your debt, or call yourself "stupid with money," what happens next? You avoid. You check out. You swipe your card again to numb the feeling. Shame does not motivate change, it fuels the exact behaviors you are trying to escape.

Self-compassion flips that. It takes the sting out of mistakes so you can actually learn from them. You don't double the damage by punishing yourself. You just notice what happened, adjust, and move forward.

Here is how it works in practice:

- **After an impulse buy.** Instead of "I am such an idiot, I will never get this right," try "That purchase did not align with what I want, but it is one data point, and now I know my weak spot better."
- **When you blow a budget.** Instead of "I am terrible with money," try "That plan was too rigid for real life. I need to design something more forgiving."
- **When you feel behind.** Instead of "Everyone else has it together but me," try "I am starting from where I am, and progress still counts even if it is slow."

This is not toxic positivity. You are not excusing bad habits or pretending everything is fine. You are creating a mental environment where change is possible instead of drowning in self-loathing.

And here's research to back this up. A 2019 study published in *Personality and Social Psychology Bulletin* found that people who practiced self-compassion were more likely to engage in healthy financial behaviors because they were less stuck in cycles of avoidance and guilt. Translation: when you stop kicking yourself, you finally have the energy to do better.

And here is the irony: the same brain that can shred you for a mistake is also the one that can learn from it if you give it space. Shame says "I blew it, so why bother." Compassion says "I blew it, so what can I try next." Only one of those sentences leads to action.

Challenge

The next time you mess up with money, and you will, because we all do… **notice your self-talk**. Catch the harsh inner voice. Then deliberately swap it for something you would say to a friend in the same situation. You would not call your friend an idiot for ordering Uber Eats when they were exhausted. You would tell them, "Rough night. Tomorrow is another chance." So why not give yourself the same baseline kindness?

Self-compassion is not just about feeling better. It is about breaking the cycle of shame and avoidance that keeps people stuck. When you see money mistakes as information instead of indictments, you can actually build momentum.

Because, remember? This is not a book on investment or 'get rich quick' advice, it's about **you and your relationship with money**.

You now have tools for emotional calm: reframing anxiety, building a dashboard, experimenting safely, and treating yourself with compassion instead of criticism. That is your safety net.

From here, we shift into identity. Part III is where you start experimenting with who you are becoming — someone who budgets out loud, someone who takes on challenges, someone who sees themselves as a builder instead of a spender.

A Tiny Favor That Helps Someone You'll Never Meet

People who share what helped them make other people's lives easier. That is the whole point of this book. If it gave you even one useful tool or insight, would you spend 60 seconds helping the next reader find it faster?

Would you help a stranger for free if it cost you one minute?

Here is how your review helps, for real:

- One more anxious spender finds calm instead of shame.
- One more person pauses before debt, not after.
- One more family gets fewer money fights and more peace.
- One more Future You fund gets started.

Your words beat my marketing. Reviews are how readers decide if this book is worth their time and cash. You are the hero here, not me.

What to write (keep it simple)

- One sentence about what changed for you.
- One tool you actually used.
- Who you would recommend it to.

That is it. No essays, minimal effort, maximal impact.

Ready?

Point your camera at the QR code:

Thank you for paying it forward. You did not just review a book. You nudged someone's money story in a better direction.

Want to Stay in Touch?

I will only ever get in touch when I write something new. No fluff, no guilt, no spam.

Join the list here:

PART III:

From Spender to Builder — Your New Money Identity

Chapter 7:

Loud Budgeting & No-Buy Challenges That Actually Stick

What Loud Budgeting Really Means (And How to Try It Without Awkwardness)

There is a new trend floating around social media called "loud budgeting." On the surface it sounds like something invented by a finance bro who wanted to make spreadsheets sexy. But at its core, it is a surprisingly powerful shift in how you talk about money.

Loud budgeting is simple. Instead of hiding your financial choices out of shame or fear of judgment, you say them out loud. You name your limits, you tell people why you are not spending, and you normalize the fact that money is not infinite. It is budgeting with the volume turned up, not whispered in the privacy of your banking app.

Here is what it looks like in practice.

- Your friend invites you to an expensive dinner, and instead of panicking and making up an excuse, you say, "I am not going out this week, I am saving for my trip."
- Your coworker suggests another round of drinks and you say, "No thanks, that is not in my budget tonight."
- Your family pressures you to pitch in for something you cannot afford, and you respond, "I am sticking to my budget right now."

That is loud budgeting. Not apologizing. Not over-explaining. Just saying the truth.

Why does this matter? Because silence is expensive. When you keep your budget private, you end up saying yes to things you cannot afford. You swipe to avoid awkwardness. You bend your financial boundaries because you are scared of looking cheap. And the end result is resentment and regret.

Loud budgeting flips that script. It takes the awkwardness out of money talk by making it normal. It also gives you accountability. Once you say "I am saving for a house deposit" out loud, you are more likely to stick to it. And here is the sneaky bonus: people respect it more than you think.

The fear is that everyone will judge you. The reality is that half the people you talk to are quietly relieved, because they wanted to say the same thing but were too scared. Loud budgeting does not just help you, it gives permission for everyone around you to stop pretending.

And yes, it will feel uncomfortable at first. We are trained to treat money as taboo. Talking about it feels like breaking some unspoken social code. But awkward is temporary, and broke is forever. If the choice is ten seconds of discomfort or another month of credit card debt, you know which one makes sense.

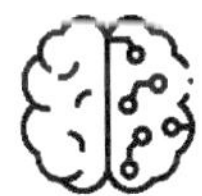

Psychology

By speaking your budget out loud, you are **reinforcing your identity** as someone who is in control of their money. This is not about "I cannot afford it, poor me." This is about "I am making intentional choices because I have goals." It is the difference between scarcity and agency.

Pro Tip
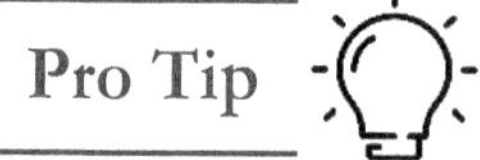

Keep your phrasing short and confident. Avoid essays. "I am budgeting right now" lands better than a long-winded explanation of your bank account. The less energy you waste justifying, the more powerful the statement becomes.

So if you are tempted to try loud budgeting, start small. Practice with safe people first, like a close friend, a partner, a sibling. Build the muscle. Over time, it will get easier to say no without guilt and yes with intention.

Because here is the bottom line: money boundaries are only as strong as your willingness to voice them. Whispering them in your head is not enough. Say them out loud, even if your voice shakes, and watch how much lighter it feels to stop carrying the weight of silent spending.

The Psychology Behind No-Buy / Low-Buy Challenges

At first glance, a "no-buy challenge" sounds like punishment. The name alone makes it feel like financial Lent all restriction, no joy. But in reality, no-buy or low-buy challenges are less about deprivation and more about rewiring your brain. They create a little lab where you get to observe your habits in action.

Here is how it usually works. You set a rule for yourself: no new clothes for 30 days, or no takeout for a month, or only groceries until payday. Sometimes it is all spending freezes, sometimes it is just one category you know is your Achilles' heel. The point is not to starve yourself of everything. The point is to draw a bright line so you can finally see the urges you usually act on automatically.

Because here is what happens when you take a break from buying: you notice the itch. The scrolling habit. The little voice that says, "I deserve this, it's only twenty bucks." You notice how often you shop out of boredom, stress, or FOMO. And once you see it, you can't unsee it. That awareness is the real win

Psychologists call this **stimulus control**. By taking the option off the table temporarily, you interrupt the loop that normally runs unchecked. It is like taking alcohol out of the house for Dry January. Suddenly you are forced to confront the emotions behind the habit instead of pouring another glass.

And here is one wild thing: most people who do no-buy or low-buy challenges report **feeling lighter, not deprived**. They realize they already own enough. They find joy in using what they have. They discover that the urge to shop passes much faster than they thought, and that not buying becomes its own kind of dopamine hit.

I once read a woman's blog about her year-long no-buy challenge. She expected it to feel like financial jail. Instead, she said the best part was not the money she saved (though that was real) but the mental quiet. No more constant decision fatigue about whether to buy. No more endless cart shuffling. Just space. She called it "the freedom of fewer choices."

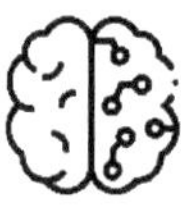

Psychology

A no-buy challenge works because it **takes away the noise**. It forces a pause long enough for you to see the difference between needs and reflexes. It is not about proving how disciplined you are. It is about resetting the baseline.

If the idea of a full freeze makes you break out in hives, that is where low-buy comes in. Low-buy is gentler: you allow spending in certain areas, but you put firm limits on the categories that drain you. It is the difference between cutting out sugar entirely and just skipping dessert most nights. Both work, but one might feel more sustainable.

Pro Tip

Write down your rules before you start. If it is all in your head, you will rationalize every loophole. "This sweater is technically a basic, so it doesn't count." Please. Put it in writing. Decide what is allowed and what isn't, set the time frame, and then track how you feel as you go.

The end goal is not to live a no-buy life forever. The end goal is to come out the other side with a new relationship to spending — one where you are in the driver's seat instead of your impulses.

But challenges alone are not enough. Some people thrive when they share their progress with others, others feel safer keeping it private. Which raises the question: what actually works better, social accountability or private wins? That is where we are headed next.

Social Accountability vs. Private Wins: Which Works Better?

Here's the million-dollar question: do you actually stick to money goals better when you shout them from the rooftops, or when you quietly grind in private like a financial Batman?

On one hand, social accountability is powerful. Tell your friends you're on a no-buy challenge, and suddenly that impulse to order a $200 air fryer at 2 a.m. has a new hurdle: the shame of having to admit it in the group chat. Humans are wired for peer pressure, and sometimes weaponizing it works. Weight Watchers has been running on this principle for decades. Same with those Instagram fitness people who post every single gym selfie, they're less about quads and more about not looking flaky online.

But here's the problem with making everything public: it can backfire spectacularly. Announce your savings goal to everyone you know, and now every relative, coworker, and random Facebook friend gets to ask "How's the house fund going?" every time you breathe. If you fall off track, it feels like a public trial. Nobody likes being cross-examined about why they caved and bought a latte.

Private wins, on the other hand, are quieter but often sweeter. There's something delicious about saying nothing, sticking to your plan, and then one day casually revealing, "Oh, yeah, I paid off my credit card last month." Boom. Mic drop. Nobody got to watch you stumble. Nobody was tracking your receipts. You did it for yourself, not the applause.

So which is better? Honestly, it depends on what motivates you more: **fear of embarrassment** or **smug inner satisfaction**. If being held accountable by others lights a fire under you, go loud. If you'd rather dodge the peanut gallery and enjoy the shock reveal later, stay quiet. Both work. The trick is knowing **your** wiring.

Want a hybrid? Try telling just one trusted friend, the kind of person who will hype your wins and check in when you flake, not the type who will turn it into gossip fodder. That way you get accountability without feeling like you're starring in a reality show *Broke and Afraid.*

Here's the key: whether you go public or private, pick one and own it. Waffling between the two is where people trip, they announce their goals, then ghost when it gets hard, then feel too ashamed to restart. That's how resolutions die. Decide whether you thrive on an audience or you thrive in the shadows, and then stick with that path.

Because at the end of the day, nobody cares about your budgeting drama as much as you do. They're too busy worrying about their own. Which is freeing, if you think about it.

Now, even if you nail loud budgeting and challenges, there's one sneaky enemy waiting in the wings: rebound spending. That lovely moment when you go six weeks without shopping, feel like a financial monk, and then blow it all in a single weekend.

How to Avoid the Backlash of "Rebound Spending"

This is the dark side of every no-buy challenge, budgeting streak, or money detox: the rebound. You spend weeks being virtuous, stacking up little wins, patting yourself on the back for your monk-like restraint. And then one day you snap. You go "just browsing" at Target and come home $300 poorer with a cart full of scented candles and throw pillows that don't match anything you own.

That's rebound spending. It's the financial version of crash dieting. You restrict hard, feel proud for a while, and then binge because the deprivation was too intense.

Why does it happen? Because willpower is a limited resource. When you push too hard, too long, without any release valves, your brain eventually rebels. It doesn't whisper, it shouts: "Screw this, I want everything now." And you give in, not just a little, but a lot.

So how do you stop the backlash? You build in pressure valves before you explode.

1. Budget for joy on purpose. If you plan zero fun money, your brain will manufacture rebellion. Give yourself a small, guilt-free fund each month to blow however you want. A book, a coffee, a Friday night takeout. The point is not the amount, it is the permission.

2. Swap the binge with a mini splurge. Instead of going from saint to sinner overnight, add little controlled splurges. For example, after a no-buy month, allow one intentional purchase you actually love. That scratches the itch without burning down your progress.

3. Watch your language. If your budget sounds like prison — "I can't buy this, I'm not allowed that", your brain will start looking for an escape tunnel. Reframe it as choice. "I don't buy this because I'm saving for Europe" feels powerful, not restrictive.

4. Track the hangover. The best cure for rebound spending is remembering how awful it feels the next day. Keep a note in your phone: "Last binge: $180 on crap I didn't need, felt like garbage." Read it next time you're about to repeat the cycle.

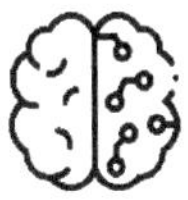

Psychology

Restriction without relief leads to rebellion. If you want consistency, you need balance. Think of it like eating. The person who eats a slice of cake once in a while is fine. The person who bans cake completely eventually eats the whole bakery until they vomit cake.

But I've got some good news for you too: **rebound spending is not proof you "failed."** It is proof your system was too rigid. Adjust the system, add some pressure valves, and you will stop ricocheting between extremes.

So the takeaway is this: aim for sustainable, not saintly. Money habits that feel human will last. Money habits that feel like punishment will eventually blow up.

And that brings us to the next big step. Here's where we zoom out and design something sturdier: **your own dashboard for peace and wealth**. Chapter 8 is about turning data into calm instead of panic.

Chapter 8:

Designing Your Reality Dashboard

(The Anti-Anxiety Money + Wealth View)

What to Track (and What to Ignore) for Financial Peace

Most people hate tracking their money because they make it way too complicated. They build spreadsheets with 47 categories, color codes, pivot tables, and then abandon the whole thing after two weeks because it feels like doing unpaid homework. Tracking your money does not need to feel like balancing the budget for NASA. It just needs to give you clarity without making your eyes bleed.

Here's what's important: some numbers matter, and some are just noise. If you try to track everything, you will drown. The secret is knowing what to pay attention to and what to ignore.

What to track:

- **Where your money goes.** Not every single gum packet, but your big categories: housing, food, transport, subscriptions, fun. If you do not know where your money is going, you are flying blind.
- **Your recurring bills.** Anything that hits monthly is worth tracking, because those quiet little leaks add up faster than you think. Five subscriptions at ten bucks each is not "just coffee money." It is six hundred dollars a year.
- **Debt balances.** You need to know how much you owe, and what the interest rates are. Ignoring debt is like ignoring a weird smell in your house. It will not go away just because you avoid it.
- **Savings and progress toward goals.** Watching your emergency fund grow or your debt shrink is like weight loss before-

and-after photos. The numbers are proof that small actions add up.

What to ignore:

- **Hyper-detailed categories.** You do not need to separate "groceries" from "toiletries" from "cleaning products" from "random impulse chocolate bar." Call it all "groceries" and move on.
- **Your daily net worth.** Checking your investments every day is like weighing yourself after every bathroom break. It is pointless, and it makes you crazy.
- **Other people's numbers.** Stop comparing your budget to some stranger's on TikTok who claims to live on thirty dollars a week. They are either lying, starving, or leaving out the part where their parents pay the bills.

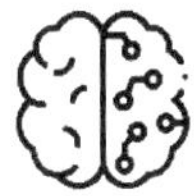

Psychology

Anxiety multiplies in vagueness, but so does burnout when you overcomplicate things. The sweet spot is tracking just enough to stay aware, not so much that it becomes a second job.

Think of it like brushing your teeth. Quick, repeatable, basic hygiene. Not a full dental surgery every night.

Because the goal of tracking is not to become a human calculator. The goal is peace. You want to open your system, see the big picture, and think, "Okay, I get it. I know where my money is going. I am not in the dark." Clarity, not torture.

Pro Tip

Your tracking system should take **less than fifteen minutes a week.** That's it. If it takes longer, you will quit. Use an app, a notebook, or a Google Sheet with five categories max. The tool does not matter. What matters is that you will actually stick with it.

And once you know what to track and what to ignore, the next step is turning that data into something you can actually act on. A simple stoplight system that tells you when to relax, when to be cautious, and when to slam the brakes.

Building Your Personal Stoplight System (Green, Yellow, Red Zones)

Numbers are boring (for the majority of the population). Colors are not. That is why a stoplight system works better than a spreadsheet full of decimals. It gives your brain something simple: green means go, yellow means caution, red means stop. No calculator required.

The idea is to translate your financial reality into three easy zones you can see at a glance. Because what freaks most people out is not the numbers themselves, it is the question, *"Am I okay right now, or am I about to screw myself?"* The stoplight system answers that in three seconds.

Here is how you build it:

Green Zone: Safe, steady, chill.

- You are paying all your bills on time.
- You have at least a small buffer in savings.
- Spending on fun stuff is guilt-free because essentials are covered.
- Nothing feels like a panic.

Yellow Zone: Warning, pay attention.

- Your buffer is getting thin. Maybe you are dipping into savings for bills or relying on credit more than usual.
- Debt payments are starting to feel heavy.
- You are not in full crisis, but if nothing changes, you could tip into red.

Red Zone: Full stop.

- Bills are at risk of being missed.
- Credit cards are maxed or close.
- No savings, no cushion, and stress is keeping you up at night.
- Every purchase feels like gambling.

The beauty here is that you do not need a degree in finance to know which zone you are in. You just need a few simple markers. For example: if you have one month of expenses covered, you are at least in yellow moving toward green. If you are covering rent with credit cards, you are in red.

Why does this work? Because your brain loves simplicity. In a study published in *Organizational Behavior and Human Decision Processes* (2016), researchers found that people make better decisions when choices are grouped into categories. A color system reduces mental load. You are no longer drowning in numbers, you are just asking, "Am I green, yellow, or red?"

You can even set this up visually. A whiteboard with three boxes. A traffic light graphic in your notes app. A color-coded spreadsheet if you insist on being fancy. The form does not matter. The colors do.

And here's the sneaky upside: the stoplight system also changes your language. Instead of saying "I'm broke," you can say, "I'm in yellow right now, working toward green." It reframes your situation as temporary, not permanent. That shift matters. Shame keeps you stuck. A framework gives you motion.

Challenge

Design your stoplight system this week. Write down what green, yellow, and red look like for you. Then update it once a week. That way, instead of guessing where you stand, you will have a flashing color-coded sign telling you exactly what's up.

Once you have your stoplight system, the next step is widening the lens. It is not just about surviving the month. It is about adding a wealth perspective — tracking net worth, savings rate, and your Future-Self Fund so you can see progress over years, not just weeks.

Adding a Wealth Lens: Net Worth, Savings Rate, and Future-Self Fund

Up to now, we have focused on keeping you calm in the day-to-day, like paying bills, avoiding panic, making sure the rent clears without a meltdown. That is survival mode. Important, yes, but not the whole story. At some point you have to zoom out and ask the bigger question: *am I actually building wealth, or just running in place?*

This is where the wealth lens comes in. It is less about what happened this week and more about the trajectory of your life. Three simple numbers give you that lens: net worth, savings rate, and your Future-Self Fund.

Net Worth: The Big Snapshot

This is the scoreboard. Net worth is **everything you own minus everything you owe**. House, car, retirement accounts, savings — subtract the debt, and whatever is left is your number. Do not freak out if it is small or even negative at first. A lot of people start that way. The point is to track it consistently. Watching it move upward, even slowly, is the long-term proof you are moving forward.

Savings Rate: The Engine

Your savings rate is **how much of your income you actually keep**. If you earn $5,000 a month and save $500, that is a 10 percent savings rate. The higher this number, the faster you build freedom. Forget comparing yourself to some finance blogger who brags about saving 70 percent of their income while living in a cabin with no running water. Start where you are, bump it slowly, and treat progress as the win.

Future-Self Fund: The Identity Anchor

This is my favorite. The Future-Self Fund is a **separate account** that exists purely for the version of you that is five, ten, or twenty years down the line. It could be a retirement account, a brokerage account, even a simple high-interest savings account at first. The point is not the size of it. The point is that it exists, with your name on it, quietly growing. Every deposit is a love letter to the person you are becoming.

Why these three numbers? Because together they give you a bigger perspective than day-to-day budgeting ever will. Net worth tells you if the ship is moving forward. Savings rate tells you how fast. Future-Self Fund reminds you who you are building for.

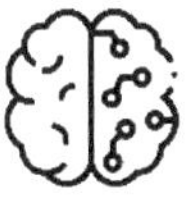

Psychology

When you zoom out to these numbers, you stop obsessing over tiny wins or losses. Overspent by fifty bucks this week? Annoying, sure, but if your net worth is still trending upward, you are fine. Missed your budget on groceries? Who cares, if your savings rate is climbing steadily. The wealth lens keeps you from spiraling over small mistakes because you see the long-term arc.

Challenge

Set up a simple tracker for these three numbers. Update once a month, not daily. Monthly is enough to see the story without stressing over every blip. Write it down in your dashboard. Celebrate small progress.

Because peace comes from knowing the little messes do not derail the big picture. And wealth, when you strip away the noise, is just those three numbers trending in the right direction over time.

Once you have the wealth lens, the final step is turning that data into action. Because knowing your numbers is great, but knowing how to actually make decisions from them is what changes your life.

Turning Data Into Decisions (Not Panic)

Here's the problem with numbers: they look objective, but the second you see them, your brain starts panicking. You open your account balance and instead of calmly thinking, *"Okay, I have $1,327 today,"* you immediately spiral into *"Oh my god, that's not enough, I'm screwed, I'll never retire, I need a startup stat!!"*

The goal of your Reality Dashboard and wealth lens isn't to flood you with data. It's to give you **decision fuel.** Numbers are not meant to be a horror show. They are meant to help you act.

So how do you keep the data useful instead of anxiety-inducing? You filter it through three questions:

1. Is this a red, yellow, or green situation?

Instead of freaking out over every dip, place the data in your stoplight system. If you're in green, relax. If you're in yellow, adjust. If you're in red, hit pause on spending and make a plan. That one frame prevents you from spiraling into "everything is doomed" mode when really, you just need to tighten a category.

2. Does this trend matter in the long run?

Your net worth dipping $300 this month because your car needed new tires? That sucks, but it doesn't matter in the wealth arc if your savings rate is still climbing. Your retirement account dipping 2 percent because the market burped? Not relevant. Focus on the direction over time, not the daily wiggles.

3. What is the smallest action I can take right now?

When the numbers feel overwhelming, the cure is micro-moves. Cancel one subscription. Transfer $20 to savings. Cook dinner instead of ordering in. Action cuts through anxiety. Waiting for the perfect plan just prolongs the panic.

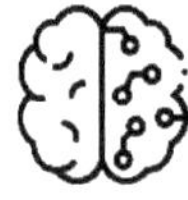

Psychology

Your nervous system hates uncertainty more than it hates bad news. When you take a scary number and connect it to a clear action, you're teaching your brain that you are not helpless. That shift — from panic to plan — is what builds resilience.

Pro Tip

Write down your go-to actions for each zone in advance. If you're in green, maybe your action is to increase savings by a tiny amount. If you're in yellow, it's cutting back in one category for the month. If you're in red, it's pausing non-essential spending for two weeks while you regroup. Having a pre-set menu of moves means you don't have to make decisions while panicked, which is when humans make the worst decisions possible.

And here's what's interesting: data without decisions is just stress. But data with action is progress. Your numbers stop being scary when they're connected to a move you can actually make today.

And with that, you've built the full dashboard: what to track, how to interpret it, how to zoom out with a wealth lens, and how to turn all of it into calm, practical decisions. That is how you stop numbers from owning you and start owning them.

Next up, Chapter 9, where we talk about the boring, unsexy, but wildly effective path to wealth. No lottery tickets, no trading schemes, just behavior that beats genius every single time.

Chapter 9:

The Boring Path to Wealth: Why Behavior Beats Genius

Why Most People Fail at Investing (Fear, Greed, and FOMO)

First and foremost let's get one thing out of the way: investing isn't rocket science. The math is boringly simple. Buy diversified stuff, keep buying it, let it sit for a long time. Done. So why do so many people fail at it? Because investing is not actually a math problem. It is a psychology problem.

Fear, greed, and FOMO are the three horsemen of investing screw-ups.

Fear is what makes people pull their money out of the market the second things dip. Your balance goes down 10 percent and suddenly your brain screams *"We're going to zero! Cash out before we lose it all!"* So you sell at the bottom, lock in your losses, and then sit on the sidelines while the market recovers without you. This is the financial equivalent of bailing out of a roller coaster on the first drop. Painful and unnecessary.

Greed is the other side of the coin. Markets are hot, your coworker is bragging about their crypto gains, and suddenly you feel like you are missing out on the gold rush. So you dump your savings into whatever is shooting up, convinced you are a genius for getting in early. Then the bubble pops, your "can't lose" stock tanks 80 percent, and you are left wondering why you thought buying Dogecoin at the peak was a good idea. Greed blinds you to risk, and risk always collects its bill.

FOMO is the cocktail of both. Fear of missing out makes you chase trends you don't understand just because everyone else is talking about them. Meme stocks, NFTs, the latest "sure thing" your friend swears is going to 10x. FOMO convinces you that sitting still is losing, when in reality sitting still is usually the smartest move.

Professional investors know this. They are counting on regular people panicking, chasing, and bailing. That is literally how they make money. When you sell low because you are scared, someone else is buying cheap. When you buy high because you are greedy, someone else is happily offloading to you. You are not playing against the market, you are playing against your own emotions.

The good news is that you do not need to outsmart Wall Street. You just need to outsmart your own brain. And that means building systems that keep you from reacting to every wiggle. Automating investments. Setting rules you do not break. Reminding yourself that short-term chaos is normal and that the long-term trend is your friend.

Most people do not fail at investing because they picked the wrong fund. They fail **because they could not sit still.** Patience beats brilliance. Calm beats clever. The investors who win are not the ones with the hottest tips. They are the ones who stay in their seats when everyone else is running for the exits.

Which brings us to the quiet, unsexy math that actually builds wealth: compounding. It is not glamorous, it is not clickbait, but it is the single most powerful force in personal finance. And if you get it, you will stop chasing shiny things and start letting time do the heavy lifting.

Compounding: The Quiet Math Behind Every Wealth Story

If there were a cheat code for building wealth, compounding would be it. The problem is that it is the least sexy concept in all of finance. It is slow, it is boring, and it does not give you anything dramatic to brag about at dinner parties. But it works, and it works better than almost anything else.

Here is the idea in plain English: compounding is **your money making more money**, and then that money making even more money. It is the financial version of gossip. Once it starts spreading, it multiplies faster than you expect.

Say you invest $1,000 and it grows 10 percent. Now you have $1,100. Next year, you earn 10 percent not just on the original $1,000, but on the $1,100. Suddenly you are making interest on your interest. Over time, that snowball effect turns small, boring deposits into shocking totals.

Albert Einstein supposedly called compounding the "eighth wonder of the world." Whether he actually said that is debatable, but the point stands: people underestimate it because it feels too simple. We want dramatic wins. Compounding delivers sneaky ones.

Here is a quick reality check. If you invest $200 a month starting at age 25 and keep going until age 65, with an average 7 percent return, you end up with around $500,000. Do the exact same thing but start at 35, and you have less than half that. Same money, same return, ten years later, a $250,000 difference. The only variable was time.

That is why compounding is both powerful and infuriating. The power is obvious: it does the heavy lifting for you if you just start and stay consistent. The frustration is also obvious: the real magic only shows up after years, sometimes decades. Which is why people give up too soon. They plant the seed, get bored when it is still a twig, and rip it out to chase something shinier.

Here is the takeaway: wealth is rarely built in big, dramatic moments. It is built in boring, repetitive deposits that compound quietly in the background. Every extra month you leave your money in the market, every reinvested dividend, every automatic contribution — it is all part of the snowball rolling downhill.

Compounding rewards patience and punishes impatience. You cannot hack it, you cannot fast-forward it, and you cannot fake it. The only thing you control is whether you start early and stick with it.

So yes, compounding is dull. But it is the kind of dull that turns ordinary people into millionaires while the thrill-seekers are still trying to time the next big thing.

Once you understand compounding, the next step is protecting it. Because the real trick is not finding the perfect investment, it is showing up consistently. And that is where psychology kicks in again: how do you stay steady long enough for the snowball to do its work?

The Psychology of Consistency: Small, Boring Wins That Grow Big

If compounding is the cheat code for wealth, consistency is the controller in your hands. Without it, the game does not play. And here's the part nobody likes to hear: **consistency is not glamorous**. It is not buying crypto at the exact bottom or flipping a house in a weekend. It is setting up an automatic transfer and letting it run while you live your life.

Most people fail here because they confuse exciting with effective. They want fireworks. They want the big moment where everything changes overnight. But money growth is more like brushing your teeth. It feels boring and pointless on any given day, but skip it long enough and things get ugly.

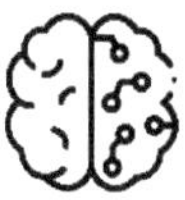

Psychology

Your brain craves novelty, so routine feels dull. Which is why sticking with a long-term plan feels like trudging through bland oatmeal. But consistency is how the snowball of compounding keeps rolling. Every little, repeated action adds weight. One skipped transfer does not matter, but a **habit** of skipping them kills momentum.

Think about it like exercise. Nobody gets fit from one heroic workout. You get fit from showing up again and again, even when it is not Instagram-worthy. Same with money. Most of us don't build wealth by hitting one jackpot. You build it by making dozens of small deposits, month after month, while everybody else quits because it feels too boring.

Here's where **automation** saves you. By taking the decision out of your hands, you remove the temptation to "forget" or "wait until next month." An automatic savings transfer does not care if you are tired, stressed, or hungover. It just happens. And over time, those tiny, boring moves pile up into something impressive.

The truth is, consistency beats intensity. The person who invests $200 every month for 20 years ends up way ahead of the person who invests $5,000 once and then never again. That is because the consistent habit keeps feeding the snowball, while the one-time splash just sits there melting.

I once heard someone describe wealth-building as "controlled monotony," and honestly, that's perfect. The people who win are the ones willing to lean into the monotony. They accept that it is not thrilling most days, but they know the thrill comes later when the numbers finally pop.

Challenge

Find one tiny money habit you can repeat without effort. It might be rounding up your purchases into savings, or transferring $50 every payday, or checking your Reality Dashboard once a week. Keep it small enough that it feels almost laughably easy, then do it over and over.

Because the small, boring wins are not boring at all once you zoom out. They are the whole game. And if you stick with them, they grow big in ways that will shock you.

Which brings us to the final piece of this chapter: the Freedom Formula. The simplest, least sexy, most effective path to wealth ever written. It is the financial equivalent of "eat your vegetables." You already know it, but actually doing it changes everything.

The Freedom Formula: Spend Less Than You Earn, Automate the Rest

Here it is, the entire secret to wealth boiled down into one sentence: **spend less than you earn and automate the rest.** That's it. That's the formula. No viral hacks, no complicated stock-picking strategies, no "guru" courses charging $999 to reveal the obvious.

Of course, the problem is not knowing the formula. The problem is actually living it. Because spending less than you earn sounds insultingly simple, but in practice it means saying no to things you want, resisting a world designed to make you buy constantly, and choosing boring consistency over flashy chaos. And automation sounds easy too, until you realize it means giving up control and trusting systems instead of micromanaging.

So let's break it down.

Spend less than you earn.

This is the non-negotiable. If you spend more than you bring in, no investment strategy on Earth can save you. Overspending is like bailing water into your own sinking boat. You have to flip the flow. And no, it does not mean living like a monk forever. It means being honest about what you value, cutting what you don't, and making sure the math works.

Automate the rest.

This is where the magic happens. The second your paycheck hits, money should move automatically:

- A chunk to bills so they are covered.
- A chunk to savings so you have a buffer.

- A chunk to investments so Future You gets paid. What is left is yours to spend however you like, guilt-free. That is the system. Once it is set, you stop making a thousand micro-decisions every month and let the defaults do the work.

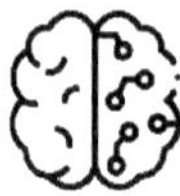

Psychology

When you automate, you **take willpower out of the equation**. You do not have to rely on motivation or discipline, both of which vanish the second you have a bad day. Systems run when you are tired, stressed, or distracted. Systems don't care if you are in the mood. They just work.

And here is the punchline: this formula is so boring that most people ignore it. They would rather chase crypto coins or obsess over the next hot stock tip than follow the dull math of spend less, save more, let time do its thing. But the people who actually stick with this boring formula are the ones who end up wealthy.

It is not about brilliance, it is not about timing, it is not about luck. It is about the quiet math of margin and momentum. Margin is the gap between what you earn and what you spend. Momentum is what happens when that gap compounds automatically over years. Put the two together and you get freedom.

That is why it is called the Freedom Formula. Not because it makes you rich overnight, but because it slowly buys you options. Options to say no to work you hate. Options to take time off without panic. Options to design your life instead of constantly reacting to bills.

So yes, it is simple. Almost offensively simple. But simple is not the same as easy. If it were easy, everyone would be financially free already. The real work is sticking with it when everything around you is screaming for you to abandon it.

And with that, we close the chapter on behavior beating genius. You now know why most people fail at investing, how compounding quietly builds wealth, why consistency is the real flex, and why the Freedom Formula is the most boring, effective plan of all.

Next, we are zooming in on the emotional side of investing: how to keep your cool when markets get rocky, how to separate fear and greed from your decisions, and how to actually build confidence without turning into a stock-obsessed maniac.

Chapter 10:

Future-Self Investing

(Confidence Without Panic or Greed)

Emotional Investing vs. Calm Investing

Investing is supposed to be about numbers, but in reality it's mostly about feelings. People like to pretend they are rational, data-driven masterminds making calm, objective decisions, but most investing mistakes come down to raw emotion. Fear, greed, excitement, panic. You're not competing with Wall Street's algorithms. You're competing with your own amygdala.

Emotional investing looks like this:

- You panic-sell your retirement fund because the market dipped 5 percent in a week.
- You throw your savings into whatever stock is trending on Reddit because someone said "to the moon."
- You check your portfolio ten times a day and feel like your entire identity rises and falls with every tiny wiggle.

It's exhausting, and it usually ends with buying high and selling low, which is the exact opposite of what you want.

Calm investing, on the other hand, looks boring as hell. It's automatic contributions to a diversified account. It's not touching your investments when the market goes red. It's reminding yourself that the news cycle thrives on drama, and the market thrives on time. Calm investing is the financial equivalent of staying seated on a turbulent flight. The ride might get bumpy, but you know the plane isn't crashing just because the drink cart rattled.

Why is calm so powerful? Because it protects the one thing that actually makes you money: **time in the market.** Every study on investor returns says the same thing: the people who make the most money are not the ones chasing hot tips, they are the ones who left their money alone. In fact, a Fidelity report once found that the best-performing accounts were those of people who literally forgot they had an account. Dead people beat day traders.

So how do you become a calm investor?

1. **Automate it.** If you remove the need to choose every month, you remove the chance of talking yourself out of it.
2. **Shrink your exposure.** Don't check your portfolio every day. Monthly or even quarterly is plenty.
3. **Anchor yourself to history.** Markets have always had crashes. They have also always recovered. Zoom out and the line goes up.

Here's the takeaway: emotions are terrible financial advisors. If you want to win, you can't just know the numbers, you have to manage the feelings. Calm is not sexy, calm is not brag-worthy, calm doesn't get you clout online, but calm keeps your money growing while everyone else panics.

Now that we've looked at calm versus chaos in investing, let's dig deeper into the two emotions that wreck more portfolios than anything else: fear and greed.

How Fear and Greed Drive Market Mistakes

In Chapter 9 we met Fear and Greed as the drama queens of investing — the ones convincing you to bail when things get rough or to chase shiny trends when everyone else is bragging. But Fear and Greed don't just whisper "sell low, buy high." They wear disguises. They show up in your news feed, in your group chat, even in your own rational-sounding inner monologue. And that's what makes them dangerous.

Fear looks like this in real life:

- Doomscrolling headlines about "the biggest crash since 2008" and thinking your retirement account is toast.
- Obsessively refreshing your brokerage app every five minutes and feeling your stomach drop with every red tick.
- Telling yourself you're being "cautious" when really you're just panic-selling into a temporary dip.

Greed looks like this:

- Watching your coworker brag about doubling their money on crypto and feeling like an idiot for not joining in.
- Seeing TikTok "finance gurus" hype the next hot stock and convincing yourself you're just "seizing an opportunity."
- Deciding to put way too much money into one idea because diversification suddenly feels boring.

Notice the disguise: fear calls itself prudence, greed calls itself ambition. Both sound responsible, but both are just your emotions trying to drive the car while blindfolded.

These aren't abstract forces, they're wired into your brain. **Fear** is your survival instinct, the same one that told your ancestors to run from snakes. **Greed** is your dopamine system, the same one that lit up when your ancestors found a tree full of ripe fruit. Those instincts kept them alive in caves, but in markets they will bankrupt you.

So how do you fight back?

1. **Zoom out.** A market crash looks terrifying on a 1-day chart, but on a 10-year chart it looks like a speed bump.
2. **Name the disguise.** When you catch yourself saying, "I'm just being cautious," ask: is this actual risk management or just fear in a trench coat? Same for greed — is this a strategy, or am I chasing someone else's dopamine hit?
3. **Automate your moves.** Fear and Greed can't hijack decisions you already took out of their hands. That's why automatic investing is boring, but brilliant.

The point is not to eliminate Fear and Greed. You can't. They're human. The point is to recognize them, laugh at the disguises, and refuse to hand them the wheel.

Fear and Greed aren't bad characters to have in your life. They're entertaining as hell to watch on Twitter. But in your portfolio? They're the reason most people spend decades running in circles.

And that's why the antidote isn't genius or guts. It's confidence built through repetition. Small wins, stacked consistently, are what keep Fear and Greed from calling the shots.

Micro-Investing and Small Wins That Build Confidence

If fear and greed are the villains of investing, confidence is the superhero, but not the kind in a cape. More like the nerdy sidekick who quietly saves the day while everyone else is freaking out. And the fastest way to build that confidence is not by making a million dollars overnight. It is by stacking small wins until you start to trust yourself.

That is where micro-investing comes in. Micro-investing is the **practice of putting tiny amounts of money into investments**, sometimes just a few dollars at a time. Think apps that round up your coffee purchase and drop the spare change into a portfolio. Or setting up a $20 weekly transfer into an index fund. The amounts are so small that fear has nothing to grab onto. You are not risking your rent money. You are risking the cost of a burrito.

Why does this work? Because your brain learns through experience, not theory. Reading about investing might make you feel smart for five minutes, but the second the market dips, you panic because you have no skin in the game. Putting even a tiny amount into the market, watching it wiggle up and down, and realizing the world did not end, that rewires your nervous system faster than any blog post ever could.

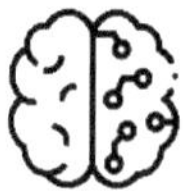

Psychology

Fear thrives on imagination. You picture losing everything, so you freeze. **Micro-investing replaces imagination with data.**

"I invested $20. The market dipped. I lost 60 cents. Nothing exploded. I'm fine." Repeat that a few times and suddenly you're calmer.

Greed gets checked, too. It's hard to fantasize about becoming a millionaire overnight when you are investing coffee money. You learn patience, because small deposits force you to zoom out. You start seeing the growth curve instead of chasing jackpots.

And the best part? Small wins snowball. You go from "I saved five bucks this week" to "I've got a hundred in this account now" to "Wait, when did this hit a thousand?" The numbers creep up quietly while your confidence grows louder.

I once knew a guy who started micro-investing with literal pocket change. At first it felt silly, like dropping coins in a jar. But within a year, his "silly little jar" had turned into a $700 investment account. It wasn't life-changing money, but it was life-changing proof. Proof that he could save. Proof that he could invest. Proof that the system worked. That proof made him comfortable ramping up his contributions, and that's when things really took off.

Challenge

Pick one micro-investing habit. Round-ups, a weekly $10 transfer, or a "skip one Uber Eats meal and invest it instead" rule. Keep it tiny and automatic. The point is not the amount. The point is the habit, the repetition, the steady drip of confidence you build every time you see the balance grow.

Because in the end, investing confidence doesn't come from striking it rich. It comes from hundreds of boring little receipts that prove you can show up, stay calm, and let the system work.

And once you have calm, consistency, and confidence built on small wins, you are ready for the ultimate upgrade: full automation. That is where you stop fiddling altogether, set the system once, and let your money grow while you go live your life.

Automating Investments: Index Funds, Dollar-Cost Averaging, and Chill

By now, you've learned that fear and greed will mess with your head, small wins build confidence, and consistency is the real flex. So how do you lock all of that in without having to babysit your portfolio every day? You automate. Because the less you touch your money, the better it behaves.

Here's the formula: **index funds + dollar-cost averaging + automation = calm wealth.**

Step one: Index funds.

Index funds are like the all-you-can-eat buffet of investing. Instead of picking one shiny stock and hoping it doesn't tank, you buy a slice of the entire market. It's diversified, cheap, and proven to work over time. You're not betting on one company's CEO not doing something stupid. You're betting on the overall economy growing, which it tends to do.

Step two: Dollar-cost averaging.

This is the practice of putting in a fixed amount of money on a regular schedule, regardless of what the market is doing. When prices are high, your dollars buy fewer shares. When prices are low, your dollars buy more. Over time, it evens out. It's like shopping during both sales and full price days, except you don't even check the calendar. You just keep buying.

Step three: Automation.

This is where the magic happens. You set up a recurring transfer that moves money from your paycheck into your investments automatically. No decision fatigue, no "should I wait until the market dips," no forgetting. It just happens while you're busy living your life.

Why is this so effective? Because it takes your messy human emotions out of the loop. You don't get the chance to panic-sell when the market dips. You don't get to FOMO-buy when the market is hot. Your system keeps chugging along while everyone else is losing their minds.

Remember, the best investors are not the ones constantly tinkering. They're the ones who set it and forget it. As I touched upon it earlier, Vanguard once studied its client accounts and found that the people with the best returns were either dead or inactive. That's true. The people who did nothing beat the people who fiddled constantly. So, set it up and keeps your paws off.

Challenge

Pick one simple index fund (broad market, low fees), set a recurring investment amount (even $50 a month is fine), and **let it run.** Don't overthink it. Don't try to time the market. Don't try to outsmart the system. Just automate and chill.

And with that, you've got the full investor toolkit: emotional calm, fear and greed awareness, confidence through small wins, and full automation with index funds. You're officially out of the panic-and-FOMO club and into the boring-but-rich one.

Now it's time to put everything together. Part IV is your six-week reset — the daily 15-minute plan that turns all these concepts into real habits. Prepare for take-off.

PART IV:

The 6-Week Money Reset

Chapter 11:

Week-by-Week Plan

(Micro Wins That Compound)

Your 15-Minute Daily Money Reset

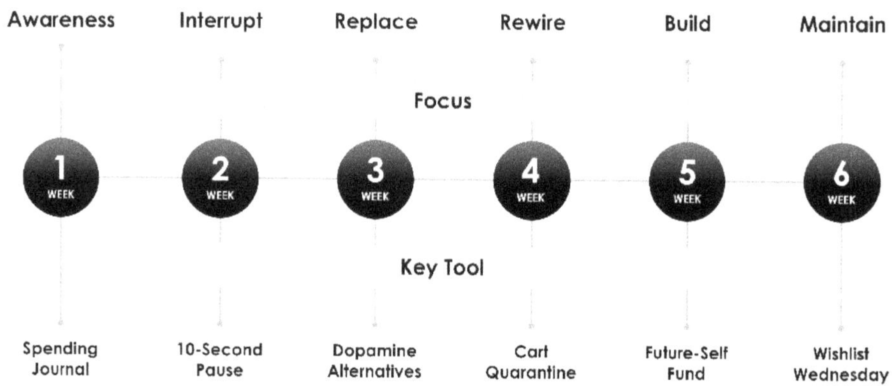

Each week builds a single habit.

Six small rewires = one major mindset shift.

Week 1: Track Without Judgment (Awareness Phase)

Theme of the week: **Building awareness without shame.**

Before you can change anything about your money, you need to see where it actually goes. Not where you *think* it goes, not where you *wish* it goes, but where those dollars actually disappear when you're tired, stressed, or three cocktails deep. The rule this week is simple: observe, don't judge. Think scientist with a clipboard, not judge in a courtroom.

Day 1 (15 min): Download & Set Up Your Tracking System

- Choose your tool: app, Google Sheet, or even Notes on your phone (5 min).
- Record today's spending in real time (10 min).

Tip: don't overthink the tool. The best system is the one you'll actually use, not the prettiest spreadsheet you never open again.

Day 2 (15 min): The Emotion Check-In

- Before every purchase, pause and ask: *"What feeling is driving this?"* (run up to 15 min in practice across the day).
- At night, jot down what came up most. Stress? Boredom? FOMO?

You'll be shocked at how often your wallet is doing therapy work your brain skipped.

Day 3 (15 min): Identify Your Spending Triggers

- Review yesterday's purchases (10 min).
- List your top three emotional or situational triggers (5 min).

Example: "Scroll TikTok after work = add to cart." Or, "Stressful meeting = ordering Uber Eats."

Day 4 (15 min): The Money Story Audit

- Write down three money messages you absorbed growing up (10 min).
- Circle which ones still influence you today (5 min).

Maybe it's "we can't afford that," or "treat yourself because life is short." The point is to see what scripts are running in the background.

Day 5 (15 min): Pattern Recognition

- Review this week's spending data (10 min).
- Highlight any recurring themes (5 min).

Example: "I keep overspending on food delivery when I'm exhausted" or "Impulse buys hit hardest when I'm scrolling late at night."

Day 6 (15 min): Weekend Spending Observation

- Track everything you buy on the weekend.
- Pay attention to social and leisure spending, it often looks different from weekday habits.

No shame, just curiosity. Weekends are sneaky budget killers.

Day 7 (15 min): Reflection & Prep for Week 2

- Write a quick summary: What did you learn about yourself this week? (10 min)
- Set an intention for Week 2 (5 min).

Example: "I want to practice pausing before I swipe."

Takeaway

You cannot fix what you cannot see.

Week 1 is about shining a light without beating yourself up. By tracking without judgment, you finally get a clean baseline.

The mistakes you notice are not failures — they are signals. And now you are ready to start interrupting those urges in Week 2.

Week 2: Interrupt the Urges (Impulse Toolkit)

Theme of the week: **Building your "pause" muscle.**

Now that you've tracked your triggers in Week 1, it's time to mess with them. Most impulse spending happens in seconds, which means you don't need hours of self-discipline, you just need a couple of seconds of space. This week is about inserting those speed bumps and learning to sit with the urge instead of instantly swiping.

Day 8 (15 min): Master the 10-Second Pause

- Every time you feel the urge to buy, stop and literally count to ten. Out loud if you have to.
- Keep a tally of how many urges came up versus how many actual purchases you made.

The goal isn't zero spending, it's awareness: proving to yourself that most "urgent" purchases dissolve if you give them a breath.

Day 9 (15 min): Cart Quarantine Setup

- Set up your 24-hour rule system: anything you want online goes into a cart or wishlist, not checkout.
- Test it with one item today.

Pro tip: half of those carts will start looking stupid in the cold light of tomorrow morning.

Day 10 (15 min): The Substitution Experiment

- When the urge hits, try three free or cheap alternatives: take a walk, text a friend, make a coffee.
- At night, rate which substitution worked best.

This isn't about denying yourself forever. It's about giving your brain another dopamine snack that doesn't wreck your bank account.

Day 11 (15 min): Wishlist Wednesday

- Create an official wishlist document or board.
- Move five "want to buy" items there instead of purchasing.

Here's the secret: 70 percent of them will stop feeling urgent within a week. The list is your holding pen for fake "emergencies."

Day 12 (15 min): The Cost-Per-Joy Calculator

- Pick three recent purchases and calculate how many times you've used them so far.
- Divide the cost by the uses. That's your cost-per-joy.

Example: $200 shoes worn once = $200 per joy. Netflix at $15 for ten hours of bingeing = $1.50 per joy. Suddenly you'll see which "cheap" buys are actually expensive regrets.

Day 13 (15 min): Social Media Audit

- Unfollow five accounts that trigger your spending urges.

- Notice how ads and influencer posts hit your brain.

Your feed is either fueling your FOMO or giving you peace. Curate accordingly.

Day 14 (15 min): Week 2 Wins Review

- Count how many urges you successfully paused.
- Celebrate even the tiny victories.

You're not aiming for perfection. You're aiming for proof that you can interrupt the loop, even once. That proof is the muscle you'll build on.

Takeaway

Impulse spending thrives on speed.

Once you slow it down, it loses its power. Week 2 is about proving to yourself that you actually can pause, substitute, and redirect. Every time you do, you're not just saving money, you're building confidence in your ability to run the show.

Week 3: Automate & Add Friction (Systems Design)

Theme of the week: **Make good choices automatic, make bad ones annoying.**

You're not lazy. You're human. Your brain loves the path of least resistance, which means if spending is easier than saving, spending will win every single time. This week is about flipping the defaults: money flows toward your goals automatically, and overspending becomes a hassle.

Day 15 (15 min): Automate Your Savings

- Set up one automatic transfer into savings (even $5 a week counts).
- Choose the amount and frequency that feels doable without panic.

Think of this as paying Future You before anyone else gets a cut.

Day 16 (15 min): Create Spending Friction

- Delete saved payment info from three favorite shopping sites.
- Remove one shopping app from your phone.

If checkout takes effort, half your impulses will vanish before you even find your credit card.

Day 17 (15 min): The Cash Envelope Test

- Pick one category (like eating out) and try paying with cash for the day.
- Notice how much harder it is to part with physical bills than to tap plastic.

Cash hurts in a good way. That sting is your brain paying attention.

Day 18 (15 min): Environment Design Audit

- Remove spending temptations from three areas of your life (like unsubscribing from sale emails, clearing shopping bookmarks, or taking snacks off your desk).
- Add one visible cue for saving (like a photo of your goal taped inside your wallet).

You're hacking your environment to work for you, not against you.

Day 19 (15 min): The One-Click Rule

- Add mental or digital speed bumps to two frequent purchase triggers.

Example: log out of Amazon so you have to type your password each time, or make yourself write "why I'm buying this" in your notes before checkout. If it takes one click, make it three.

Day 20 (15 min): Bill Automation Setup

- Automate one recurring bill (rent, utilities, subscriptions).

- Review which bills are already on autopilot and organize the rest.

Automation frees you from juggling due dates and late fees.

Day 21 (15 min): Systems Check & Adjustment

- Review which friction walls and automations worked best this week.
- Adjust anything that was too rigid or too easy to bypass.

This is where you fine-tune your system so it fits real life instead of collapsing at the first stress test.

Takeaway

You don't need more willpower.

You need better defaults. When saving is automatic and spending takes effort, your future starts improving without daily battles.

Week 3 turns your money system into a self-driving car: safe, boring, and getting you where you want to go while you nap.

Week 4: Build Your Reality Dashboard (Spending + Wealth)

Theme of the week: **Creating calm through clarity.**

By now you've tracked, paused, and set up systems. The next step is the thing that actually quiets the panic: having a one-page snapshot that shows you where you stand. This week you'll build your Reality Dashboard, your anti-anxiety view of money.

Day 22 (15 min): Design Your Stoplight System

- Define your Green, Yellow, and Red spending zones. (10 min)
- Create simple visual cues (sticky notes, color labels, or a basic chart). (5 min)

You're giving your brain traffic lights instead of a math test.

Day 23 (15 min): Net Worth Snapshot

- Write down your assets (savings, investments, etc.). (10 min)
- Subtract your debts. (5 min)

Don't panic if the number isn't pretty. The goal is clarity, not instant bragging rights.

Day 24 (15 min): Build Your Reality Dashboard

- Combine balances, essentials, debts, and savings on one page. (15 min)

Format doesn't matter. Notebook, whiteboard, or Google Sheet. The rule: one page, everything that matters.

Day 25 (15 min): Create Your Future-Self Fund

- Open a separate account labeled "Future Me." (10 min)
- Set up a small automatic contribution (even $5 a week). (5 min)

This is your reminder that wealth isn't abstract. It has a name and an account.

Day 26 (15 min): Weekly Money Date Setup

- Pick a recurring time each week for a 15-minute money check-in. (10 min)
- Put it in your calendar and set reminders. (5 min)

The vibe: coffee date with yourself, not a tax audit.

Day 27 (15 min): Emergency Fund Check

- Calculate your ideal target (three to six months of essentials). (10 min)
- Write down where you're starting and how you'll build it. (5 min)

Even a $100 cushion is better than nothing. Progress beats perfection.

Day 28 (15 min): Dashboard Test Run

- Use your new dashboard to guide all spending decisions for the day. (15 min)

Notice how the clarity changes your behavior. Adjust the layout if something feels clunky.

Takeaway

Week 4 gives you **the calm you've been chasing**.

No more fog, no more guessing games. Your dashboard is your anchor. Every time money anxiety spikes, you can look at one page and see the truth. That clarity is worth more than any budgeting app ever sold.

Week 5: Practice Loud Budgeting or No-Buy Mini Challenge

Theme of the week: **Testing your boundaries out loud.**

You've tracked, paused, set up systems, and built your dashboard. Now it's time to practice actually living your new identity. This week is about experimenting with social accountability and self-control, either by trying "loud budgeting" or running a short no-buy challenge. Both are like financial CrossFit: uncomfortable at first, but a huge confidence builder.

Day 29 (15 min): Choose Your Challenge

- Decide which path you'll take this week: loud budgeting (speaking your limits) or no-buy (drawing a hard line). (10 min)
- Write down your rules and timeframe so you don't "accidentally" make loopholes. (5 min)

Your brain is sneaky. Put the rules in writing.

Day 30 (15 min): Loud Budgeting Day 1 or No-Buy Day 1

- Loud Budgeting: Practice saying, "That's not in my budget right now" three times today.
- No-Buy: Track all urges and redirect every purchase into your list. Awkward?

Yes. But awkward is cheaper than debt.

Day 31 (15 min): Social Scripts Practice

- Write three simple phrases you can use to decline spending invitations. (10 min)
- Test at least one today. (5 min)

Think of it as improv for your wallet. Keep it short and confident.

Day 32 (15 min): Values-Based Decisions

- Before every spending, ask: "Does this match my actual values?" (15 min)
- For No-Buy, focus on substituting free or cheap joy instead.

Turns out "value" is not just a marketing buzzword, it's the filter that makes decisions easier.

Day 33 (15 min): Accountability Partner Check-In

- Share your progress with a friend, partner, or journal if you're going solo. (10 min)
- Celebrate any wins, even if it's just "I didn't buy the dumb gadget today." (5 min)

Accountability works better when it's kind, not judgmental.

Day 34 (15 min): Reframe & Redirect

- Catch one FOMO moment and reframe it as "I'm saving for what matters." (5 min)

- If you're on no-buy, swap the urge for something low-cost or free. (10 min)

This is the mental judo that keeps you in the fight.

Day 35 (15 min): Challenge Reflection

- Write down what you learned about yourself this week. (10 min)
- Plan how to adapt these tools beyond the challenge. (5 min)

This isn't about surviving seven days. It's about proving you can live by choice, not by impulse.

Takeaway

Week 5 is where you practice **living your money values out loud.**

Whether you go the loud-budgeting route or the no-buy challenge, you're teaching your brain that saying no is not the end of the world. It's just a muscle you build, one awkward conversation or one skipped purchase at a time.

Week 6: Future-Self Planning (Simple Wealth System Setup)

Theme of the week: **Building sustainable wealth habits.** You've tracked, paused, built systems, and tested your boundaries. Now it's time to zoom out and put Future You in the driver's seat. The goal isn't just to avoid panic spending. The goal is to build a money life that keeps working even when you're tired, distracted, or over it.

Day 36 (15 min): Investment Account Setup

- Research and open a simple investment account (retirement account, index fund, or micro-investing app). (10 min)
- Put in any amount, even $10, to break the seal. (5 min)

You don't need to be Warren Buffett. You just need to get started.

Day 37 (15 min): Dollar-Cost Averaging Plan

- Decide on a recurring investment amount that feels safe (even $25 per month). (10 min)
- Set it to run automatically. (5 min)

Your new mantra: boring is profitable.

Day 38 (15 min): The Compound Interest Visualization

- Use a calculator (apps, Google, back of a napkin) to see how your money could grow over 10–20 years. (10 min)

- Create a simple visual reminder (screenshot, sticky note, or phone wallpaper). (5 min)

Watching $25 turn into thousands over time is proof that Future You is worth betting on.

Day 39 (15 min): Wealth Mindset Journal

- Write one page on how your relationship with money feels now compared to six weeks ago. (15 min)

Document your identity shift. This is you becoming the calm builder instead of the anxious spender.

Day 40 (15 min): Long-Term Goal Setting

- Write down one money goal for the next six months. (10 min)
- Break it into three tiny weekly steps. (5 min)

Future You doesn't need a 30-year plan. Future You just needs consistent progress.

Day 41 (15 min): System Maintenance Plan

- Decide which daily habits from the reset you'll continue long-term. (10 min)
- Create a recurring calendar reminder to check in on your dashboard once a week. (5 min)

This is the glue that keeps all your progress from slipping.

Day 42 (15 min): Graduation & Next Steps

- Write a short "contract" with yourself for how you'll keep resetting as life changes. (10 min)
- Celebrate your 42-day transformation in whatever way feels good that isn't buying more stuff you don't need. (5 min)

Congrats, you've officially reset your money identity.

Takeaway

Week 6 is about turning six weeks of practice **into a lifestyle.**

Future You is no longer a vague concept that makes you anxious. Future You now has accounts, systems, habits, and receipts.

And the beauty of this setup is that you don't have to keep fighting every day. The systems run in the background, while you get to live your life with way less stress.

Wrapping Up the 6-Week Reset

Now let's zoom out. In the past six weeks, you've gone from money fog to money clarity, from impulse autopilot to intentional control, from anxious spender to calm builder. And you did it in 15 minutes a day. No giant spreadsheets. No shame. No finance degree required.

Here's what you actually built:

- **Week 1:** Awareness without shame. You saw your patterns clearly.
- **Week 2:** The pause muscle. You learned to interrupt urges before they ran the show.
- **Week 3:** Systems that work while you're distracted. Automation and friction walls that keep you safe.
- **Week 4:** A one-page dashboard that shuts down panic with clarity.
- **Week 5:** Boundary-setting out loud. Loud budgeting or no-buy challenges that gave you real-world confidence.
- **Week 6:** A future-proof wealth system. Small investments, compound interest, and habits that will quietly stack in your favor.

That is the book's promise, delivered. A complete wealth-building system, in daily 15-minute micro-steps, designed for actual humans with actual lives. You now have receipts that it works, not because you read about it, but because you lived it for six weeks.

The beauty of this system is that it is **renewable**. You can run it again whenever life shifts, or just keep certain weeks in rotation as tune-ups. The important part is that you've proven to yourself that financial calm and progress don't require 24/7 hustle. They require small, repeatable actions, stacked over time.

This is the point where most "money books" would say, "Congrats, you're done!" But I don't write generic, I aim to deliver maximum value for your money (pun intended, *wink). So, no, you're not done. Because this isn't just about habits, it's about identity. The biggest shift is who you are becoming. Which takes us to the final chapter.

Now that the reset is complete, we turn to the reflection. Chapter 12 is about the real payoff: who you become when money anxiety is gone, how to design a money philosophy that feels like freedom, and how to make sure you don't get stuck in the perfectionist trap of managing money "perfectly."

Chapter 12:

Reflection: Who You Become When Money Anxiety Is Gone

Identity Shift: From "I'm Bad With Money" → "I'm a Calm Builder"

Here's the secret about money: most people aren't held back by math. They're held back by identity. If you've spent your whole adult life saying things like "I'm just bad with money" or "I'm terrible at saving," guess what? Your brain believes you. And when your brain believes something about your identity, your habits line up to prove it true.

Identity is sticky. If you think of yourself as "a spender," you will unconsciously make choices that reinforce that story. If you think of yourself as "someone who panics at bills," you will keep dodging the mailbox. And if you think of yourself as "financially hopeless," you'll treat every attempt to change like a doomed experiment.

So here's the reframe: you don't need to be a genius investor or a budgeting wizard. You just need a new identity. A small, believable upgrade.

Instead of *"I'm bad with money,"* try *"I'm learning to track my money."*
Instead of *"I can't save,"* try *"I'm someone who moves a little to savings every payday."*
Instead of *"I'll never get out of debt,"* try *"I'm building systems that chip away at debt every month."*

Small identity shifts are powerful because they change the question your brain asks. Old you asks, *"Why am I such an idiot with money?"* New you asks, *"What would a calm builder do here?"* Same situation, different identity, completely different decision.

And you already proved this to yourself in the 6-week reset. You tracked without judgment. You paused before spending. You built a dashboard. You automated bills. You even created a Future-Self Fund. That's not what "bad with money" people do. That's what calm builders do.

Think about it: **you now have systems that run without you**. You have proof you can make decisions without spiraling. You've practiced saying no out loud without the world ending. That is not "bad with money." That is financial competence in action.

The identity shift doesn't happen because the numbers changed overnight. It happens because you behaved your way into a new story. Your nervous system now has receipts that you **can** handle money like an adult without drama.

Challenge

Drop the old label. Retire "I'm bad with money." It doesn't serve you anymore. Replace it with something that matches the evidence you've just built. Something like:

- "I'm calm around money."
- "I'm a builder, not a spender."
- "I make small moves that compound into big results."

Say it out loud if you have to. Write it on a sticky note. Put it in your phone.

Identity is built by repetition. The more you repeat it, the more it becomes true, because your brain is annoyingly obedient when it comes to confirming its own stories.

And this is the real win: you don't have to become someone different. You already did. You just need to claim it.

Case File 04

Jamie and the Quiet Rebuild

Jamie, 31, worked in customer service and had what she called a "self-care spending habit." When stress hit, she didn't drink or gamble, she jumped online and shopped. Skincare, candles, yet another pastel journal that would end up half-filled. It felt harmless until she realized she'd blown **$480 in one month** on "little treats" that didn't actually make her feel cared for.

Her pattern was pure *emotional substitution*: she was buying calm instead of creating it. We replaced the ritual, not the reward. For 30 days, every time she wanted to buy something "for herself," she transferred the same amount into a **Future-Self Fund** labelled *Peace Money*. She paired it with a nightly 10-minute decompression routine: music, stretching, tea, so her brain still got its dopamine hit.

By week six, she had **$720 saved** and an entirely new association with self-care. "It's weird," she said. "Watching that number grow gives me the same comfort shopping used to, but it lasts."

That's the quiet magic of rewiring: the goal isn't to suppress emotion; it's to redirect it toward something that actually restores you.

Designing a Money Philosophy That Feels Like Freedom

Okay, you've survived the hacks, the dashboards, the awkward "sorry, not in my budget" convos, and even the terrifying experiment of looking at your real numbers. Now it's time to graduate **from tactics into philosophy**, your personal money operating system. And no, not philosophy like "sit in a robe quoting Marcus Aurelius while eating lentils." I mean the simple set of rules that makes your money life feel calm, aligned, and actually doable long-term.

So, the secret is: your money philosophy is not about copying someone else's. Dave Ramsey has his. TikTok finance bros have theirs. Your parents probably had one ("buy a house, pray it appreciates, never talk about credit cards"). But those aren't your rules anymore. Your money philosophy has to fit *your* life, or you'll never stick to it.

A money philosophy that feels like freedom is basically your financial autopilot script. It answers the questions:

- How do I spend without guilt?
- How do I save without misery?
- How do I build wealth without obsessing?
- And most importantly: how do I know when "enough" is actually enough?

Maybe your philosophy is: *"I spend on experiences, not clutter."* Or: *"I save 20 percent before I touch the rest, then I don't apologize for buying lattes."*
Or: *"If it doesn't add joy now or freedom later, it's not worth my money."*

Notice what's missing: shame. A good philosophy is rooted in values, not punishment. It's not "I'm not allowed to buy shoes." It's "I choose not to, because I want my money to do X instead." That tiny shift is everything. Restriction feels like prison, when values feel like freedom.

And look, you're allowed to rewrite this philosophy as you grow. What feels right in your 30s might not be what you need in your 40s. Maybe your guiding rule today is *"Get out of debt and build a cushion."* In ten years, it could be *"Max flexibility, minimal overhead."* Philosophies evolve. The point is that you're steering, not drifting.

Here's the therapist-y encouragement part: you are already more capable than you think. You've done the 6-week reset. You've built systems, faced fears, and interrupted patterns that most people never even question. You've got receipts. Now it's about claiming ownership of the whole thing and saying, "This is how I do money. These are my rules."

Because at the end of the day, freedom doesn't come from hitting a magic number in your bank account. Freedom comes from clarity and choice. When your philosophy lines up with your values, you stop second-guessing every transaction. You spend without spiraling, you save without obsessing, you invest without panic. That's peace.

So, here's your next move: write one sentence that sums up your money philosophy. Don't overthink it. Keep it messy, funny, human. Something like, *"I spend on books, save for freedom, and ignore people who think I need a designer couch."* That's it. That's your North Star.

Once you've built a money philosophy, the real trick is not falling into the perfectionist trap of trying to live it flawlessly. Because surprise:

you won't. And if you turn your philosophy into another rigid rulebook, you'll hate it and yourself. Which is why the next section is all about how to dodge that exact trap.

Avoiding the Perfectionist Trap in Money Management

Once you've got a shiny money system, the biggest risk isn't screwing it up, it's obsessing over it. Perfectionism is sneaky like that. It whispers, *"If I don't track every single cent perfectly, I'm failing."* Or *"If I miss one savings transfer, I've ruined everything."* And before you know it, you've turned your calm, practical money reset into another source of anxiety.

That's the perfectionist trap: treating money management like it's a fragile art project that only "counts" if it's flawless. Spoiler: it never will be. Life is messy. You'll miss payments. You'll splurge on something dumb. You'll forget to update your dashboard for two weeks. That's not failure, that's normal.

Perfectionism is dangerous with money because it does two things:

1. **It makes you rigid.** You set rules so tight that one slip feels catastrophic. Cue shame spiral, cue overspending as "revenge" against your own rules.
2. **It steals your wins.** Instead of celebrating progress, you're busy nitpicking yourself for not doing it perfectly. You saved $500 this month? Instead of being proud, you're mad it wasn't $600.

Here's the reframe: money management is like brushing your teeth. If you skip once, your teeth don't fall out. You just pick up the toothbrush again tomorrow. Same with budgets, dashboards, automations. They're resilient. They can handle human imperfection.

So how do you avoid the trap?

- **Lower the bar.** Aim for "good enough," not flawless. Tracking 80 percent of your spending is infinitely better than tracking nothing.
- **Normalize slip-ups.** Missed a savings transfer? Cool. Move the money tomorrow. Bought something dumb? Congrats, you're human. The win is noticing, not hiding.
- **Zoom out.** Obsessing over one dumb purchase is like judging your fitness progress by one skipped workout. Look at the trend, not the blip.
- **Ban financial self-bullying.** If you wouldn't say it to a friend, don't say it to yourself. Nobody has ever saved better by screaming, "You idiot, you bought a croissant."

The truth is, perfectionism isn't about standards, it's about fear. Fear of failing, fear of judgment, fear of not being "good enough." But here's the twist: the calmer, wealthier version of you isn't perfect either. They're just consistent. They show up most of the time, and when they mess up, they don't spiral. They adjust and keep going.

So if you find yourself slipping into perfectionist mode, take a breath and repeat this: *progress, not perfect.* Then go back to doing the next small, boring thing. That's how wealth is actually built.

Now that you've freed yourself from the trap of financial perfectionism, the final step is keeping your system alive as life changes. Because money is not one-and-done, it's ongoing, and so is the reset. Which is exactly where we're headed next.

The Ongoing Reset: Tools to Revisit When Life Shifts

Life changes, jobs change, partners come and go, babies show up, markets crash, pandemics happen, and suddenly the system that worked fine last year feels like trying to wear pants two sizes too small. That doesn't mean you failed, it only means life moved.

That's why your six-week reset isn't a one-time boot camp. It's a toolkit you can pull out anytime life shifts. Think of it like a reset button on your financial nervous system.

- **New job?** Go back to Week 1 and track without judgment to see how your new income shifts your patterns.
- **Big expense hit you?** Revisit Week 3's automation and friction walls to stabilize the chaos.
- **Feeling panicky again?** Dust off Week 4's dashboard and prove to your brain that things aren't as dire as they feel.
- **Need a confidence boost?** Run a mini no-buy challenge from Week 5 and remind yourself you're in control.
- **Future feels shaky?** Jump to Week 6 and refocus on your Future-Self Fund.

The point is: you're not chained to perfection. You've got a menu of moves, levers you can pull, a system that bends with you instead of breaking.

You are never "bad with money" again. That label doesn't belong to you anymore. Because now you know that even when you stumble, you can reset. You can regroup in 15 minutes a day. You can reboot your relationship with money without shame or panic.

And that's the real freedom. Not that you'll never mess up again, you will. Not that you'll hit some perfect financial score, you won't. The freedom is knowing you don't need perfect, you just need the reset.

This book was never about turning you into a spreadsheet robot or a Wall Street trader. It was about giving you something better: calm, clarity, and confidence. Tools you can reach for whenever life throws its next curveball.

Challenge

So here's your **last challenge** before we wrap: trust that you're already different than when you started. You've got receipts. You tracked. You paused. You built systems. You set boundaries. You made moves for Future You. That is not a person who is "bad with money." That is a person with a reset button in their pocket — someone who can keep building, no matter what comes next.

And with that, the 6-week reset is complete. The tools are yours now. The old story — the anxious spender, the panicked avoider, the person "bad with money", that's gone. The new story is yours to write, and it starts every time you choose Future You.

Conclusion

You made it. Not just to the end of this book, but through a full tour of your brain's worst money habits, the systems that actually fix them, and a six-week reset that proved you're not doomed, you're capable. That alone is a win.

Money will always be messy. There will always be another sale, another "urgent" gadget, another market wobble, another well-meaning relative trying to tell you what to do with your paycheck. You don't win by eliminating mess. You win by having tools that let you reset when it shows up.

And now you've got them:

- The awareness to spot when you're slipping.
- The pause muscle to stop an urge in its tracks.
- The friction walls and automations that protect you when your willpower is fried.
- The dashboard that cuts through panic with clarity.
- The loud boundaries and no-buy experiments that prove you can say no and still be okay.
- The Future-Self Fund that reminds you every deposit is building a calmer, freer life.

That's not just knowledge, but identity. You're now the kind of person who has a reset button, who knows how to come back, who can make money boring and let that boring compound into freedom.

And maybe that's the best part: freedom isn't flashy. It's not yachts or Lamborghinis or manifesting millions while sipping green juice in Bali.

Real freedom is opening your banking app without your stomach dropping, buying groceries without panic or saying "no thanks, not in my budget" and feeling zero shame. It's knowing Future You is covered so Present You can sleep.

That's the gift you just gave yourself: not perfection, not riches overnight, but **peace**. And peace is what lets you build everything else.

So take this reset and keep it close. Use it when life throws you off balance, use it when fear and greed start yelling, use it when you need to remember that money isn't the enemy, it's a tool. One you can now use with calm, clarity, and a little bit of swagger.

The story isn't "I'm bad with money" anymore. The story is, *"I'm a calm builder. I know how to reset. And I'm not afraid of money anymore."*

And that's a damn good ending.

You Did It

If you've reached this page, you've finished the book, which already makes you rare. Most people never get this far.

Now you can help the next reader start their reset in case if you haven't done so earlier in the book.

Leave a quick review here:

Your words don't just help me, they help strangers you'll never meet find a little more calm with their money.

And if you want more no-fluff writing of mine straight to your in-box:

Join here:

Thank you for reading.

Go be the calm builder you already proved you are.

Author's Note

If you made it all the way here, first off: thank you. You could have been doomscrolling TikTok, impulse-buying something you don't need, or binge-watching Netflix, but instead you stuck with me through a whole book about the *Psychology of Money*. That says a lot about you, specifically, that you're ready to do money differently and you are damn serious about it.

I want you to remember one thing: this wasn't a book about becoming perfect with money. It was about becoming **calm** with money. Calm enough to pause before swiping. Calm enough to check your dashboard without spiraling. Calm enough to know you can reset anytime, no matter what life throws at you.

You don't need to follow every single step flawlessly, track every coffee or hit every savings goal on time. You just need to keep showing up, imperfectly, with the tools you've learned here. Small steps, repeated often, change everything.

So keep the reset close. Rerun it when you need to. Share it with someone you love who's struggling. And above all, trust that you are not "bad with money." **You are a builder now.**

Thank you for letting me sit with you in this part of your money story. I hope it's just the beginning of something calmer, freer, and way more fun.

Wishing you a season full of joy, clarity, and just enough sparkle, and the peace of knowing **your money is finally working for you, not against you.**

Fiercely yours,
Tali

Selected Sources & Further Reading

This book pulls from psychology, behavioral economics, and personal finance research.

If you want to dive deeper (or just prove I didn't make this stuff up), here's where to look:

Behavioral Science & Money Psychology

- Kahneman, Daniel. *Thinking, Fast and Slow.* Farrar, Straus and Giroux, 2011.
- Thaler, Richard H., and Cass R. Sunstein. *Nudge: Improving Decisions About Health, Wealth, and Happiness.* Yale University Press, 2008.
- Ariely, Dan. *Predictably Irrational: The Hidden Forces That Shape Our Decisions.* HarperCollins, 2008.
- Mullainathan, Sendhil, and Shafir, Eldar. *Scarcity: The New Science of Having Less and How It Defines Our Lives.* Times Books, 2013.
- Kahneman, Daniel, and Angus Deaton. "High income improves evaluation of life but not emotional well-being." *Proceedings of the National Academy of Sciences*, 107(38), 16489–16493, 2010.
- Tversky, Amos, and Daniel Kahneman. "Loss Aversion in Riskless Choice: A Reference-Dependent Model." *Quarterly Journal of Economics*, 106(4), 1039–1061, 1991. *(added to support the "Loss Aversion / Deep Dive" section)*

Spending, Saving & Identity

- Klontz, Brad, and Ted Klontz. *Mind Over Money: Overcoming the Money Disorders That Threaten Our Financial Health.* Broadway Business, 2009.
- Furnham, Adrian, and Argyle, Michael. *The Psychology of Money.* Routledge, 1998.
- Pape, Scott. *The Barefoot Investor.* Wiley, 2017.
- Shefrin, Hersh, and Richard H. Thaler. "The Behavioral Life-Cycle Hypothesis." *Economic Inquiry*, 26(4), 609–643, 1988. *(added to reinforce present bias and future-self concepts)*

Research & Reports Cited

- Dalbar. *Quantitative Analysis of Investor Behavior (QAIB).* Annual report, various years.
- Fidelity Investments. "Who Are the Best Investors? Dead People." Internal report, often summarized in financial media.
- American Psychological Association (APA). *Stress in America* surveys (annual, especially 2022–2023 editions).
- Reserve Bank of Australia (RBA). *Household Finances Research*, various bulletins.
- Financial Times. "BNPL users spend up to 40% more per order." 2022.
- McKinsey & Company. *The State of Consumer Finance.* 2023.

- Stanford University. *Behavioral Economics and Decision Research Lab*, 2020. *(added — supports the "Impulse vs. Pause" bar chart stats on delayed gratification)*
- Journal of Consumer Research (2020–2023). Studies on gamification and spending behavior in shopping apps like Shein and Temu.

Cultural & Modern Money Trends

- *The Guardian*, *Wired*, and *Bloomberg* — articles on TikTok finance trends, doom spending, and money dysmorphia (2021–2023).
- *Business of Fashion* and *Harvard Business Review* — reports on fast fashion, consumer psychology, and the rise of ultra-cheap shopping.
- *The Conversation.* "Herd mentality and the GameStop bubble explained." February 2021. *(added — supports the Ravi / meme-stock case)*
- *Reuters.* "Crypto crash wipes trillions off digital coin market." June 2022. *(added — supports crypto example)*
- *BBC News.* "The psychology of online shopping: how retailers use gamification to hook you." 2023. *(added — ties to Sophie's case)*
- *Wikipedia.* "Jack Whittaker (lottery winner)." Entry updated 2023.

On Habits & Behavior Change

- Clear, James. *Atomic Habits*. Penguin, 2018.
- Duhigg, Charles. *The Power of Habit: Why We Do What We Do in Life and Business*. Random House, 2012.
- Duckworth, Angela. *Grit: The Power of Passion and Perseverance*. Scribner, 2016.
- Fogg, B.J. *Tiny Habits: The Small Changes That Change Everything*. Houghton Mifflin Harcourt, 2019. *(added — supports habit-loop psychology used in the 6-week reset)*

Optional Further Reading for Behavioral-Finance Nerds

(For readers who want to go deeper into the academic side.)

- Loewenstein, George, et al. "Time Discounting and Time Preference." *Journal of Economic Literature*, 2003.
- Laibson, David. "Golden Eggs and Hyperbolic Discounting." *Quarterly Journal of Economics*, 1997.
- Vohs, Kathleen D., and Faber, Ronald J. "Spent Resources: Self-Regulatory Resource Depletion and the Impact of Spending." *Journal of Consumer Research*, 2007.

www.ingramcontent.com/pod-product-compliance
Ingram Content Group UK Ltd.
Pitfield, Milton Keynes, MK11 3LW, UK
UKHW021036270726
13967UKWH00013B/2811

9 781764 459433